YEAR 5

NUMERACY

NAPLAN*-FORMAT PRACTICE TESTS
with answers

Essential preparation for Year 5
NAPLAN* Tests in Numeracy

DON ROBENS

CORONEOS PUBLICATIONS

* These tests have been produced by Coroneos Publications independently of Australian governments and are not officially endorsed publications of the NAPLAN program

YEAR 5 NUMERACY
NAPLAN*- FORMAT PRACTICE TESTS with answers
© Don Robens 2010
Published by Coroneos Publications 2010

ISBN 978-1-921565-50-2

* These tests have been produced by Coroneos Publications independently of Australian governments and are not officially endorsed publications of the NAPLAN program

THIS BOOK IS AVAILABLE FROM RECOGNISED BOOKSELLERS OR CONTACT:

Coroneos Publications
Telephone: (02) 9624 3 977   Facsimile: (02) 9624 3717
Business Address: 6/195 Prospect Highway Seven Hills 2147
Postal Address: PO Box 2 Seven Hills 2147
Website: www. coroneos.com.au or www.basicskillsseries.com
E-mail: coroneospublications@westnet.com.au

Contents

Test 1 .... Pages 4–19

Test 2 .... Pages 20–35

Test 3 .... Pages 36–51

Test 4 .... Pages 52–67

Test 5 .... Pages 68–83

Test 6 .... Pages 84–99

Test 7 .... Pages 100–115

Test 8 .... Pages 116–131

Test 9 .... Pages 132–147

Test 10 .... Pages 148–163

Answers .... Pages 164–174

NOTE:

• Students have 45 minutes to complete a test.

• Students must use 2B or HB pencils only.

1   Look at this grid.

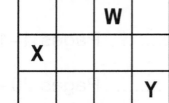

What letter is at position C4?

W   X   Y   Z
○   ○   ○   ○

2   **Danielle had 58 coloured pencils.**

She gave 23 to her brother.

How many coloured pencils did Danielle have left?

Write your answer in the box.

3   George has 8 cards. Jack has twice as many cards as George.

How many cards does Jack have?

15   16   17   18
○   ○   ○   ○

4   David bought an apple for 40c and a sandwich for 80c.

What change should David receive from $2.00?

70c   75c   80c   85c
○   ○   ○   ○

5 This graph shows the number of people voting for their favourite colour.

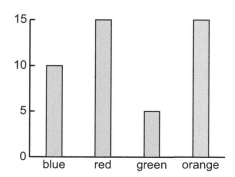

Altogether, how many people voted for their favourite colour?

25   45   35   40

○   ○   ○   ○

---

6 Sam's father is 165 cm tall.

165 cm is

○ more than 1 metre

○ equal to 1 metre

○ less than 1 metre

---

7 **Which one of these number sentences is NOT correct?**

○ 8 x 2 = 16

○ 7 x 3 = 20

○ 7 x 5 = 35

○ 3 x 10 = 30

---

8 **Circle enough of the coins below to show $2.**

$1   50c   20c   10c

20c   10c   5c

---

9 Max made this object.

Which set of shapes did Max use tomake the above object?

○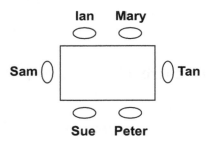

10 Rene took 59.90 seconds to run around the school playground.

This is

○ more than a minute

○ equal to a minute

○ less than a minute

11 Here is where some students sit in their classroom.

Ian   Mary
Sam ⬭ [   ] ⬭ Tan
Sue   Peter

Which one of these sentences is NOT true?

○ Peter is next to Sue.

○ Sue is opposite Ian.

○ Tan is opposite Sam.

○ Tan is opposite Mary.

12 Tony has 4 coins in his pocket. The coins add up to 80c.

How many 10c coins does he have?

13 What is the area of this shape?

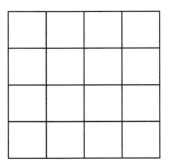

○ 20 squares ○ 18 squares ○ 16 squares

14 Colour a quarter of this shape.

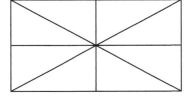

15 **Which shapes have the same perimeter?**

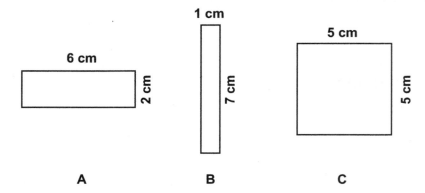

A and C   A and B   B and C

16 **Colour the hexagon.**

17 Ross has collected 99 stamps. He added another 30 stamps to his collection.

How many stamps has he now?

130   131   129   128

18 John is at **X**.

What does John see when he looks in a south-west direction?

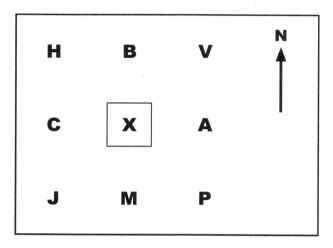

ANSWER: _____

19 There are 100 students in a library. 56 of the students are girls.

What percentage of the students are boys?

40%   45%   56%   44%

◯   ◯   ◯   ◯

20 Tammy began reading a book at 8.30. She finished reading the book in 40 minutes. **What time did she finish reading the book?**

9:15   9:20   9:10   9:05

◯   ◯   ◯   ◯

21 Sandra made 100 cards. She placed the cards into packets.

Each packet contained 11 cards.

How many cards are left over?

1   3   2   4

◯   ◯   ◯   ◯

22 Three people read the same book. They read for 15 minutes.  Shade one bubble

This tally shows how many pages they read in that time.

Names	Pages read
Tom	⑭ //
Harry	⑭ /
Jack	⑭ ⑭

Who read the most pages?

○ Tom

○ Harry

○ Jack

23 A book costs $29. Michael has a $50 note to pay for it.

How much change should he receive when he buys the book?

Write your answer in the box.

$ [   ]

24 Harry completed this graph to show the size of his friends' shoes.

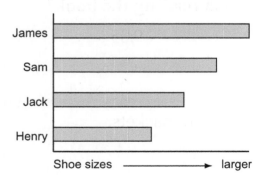

Shoe sizes ——→ larger

Who had the largest shoes?

James   Sam   Jack   Henry

   ○   ○   ○   ○

25 Elizabeth used 6 straws to make a triangular pyramid frame.

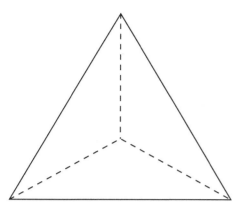

How many straws does she need to make the skeleton of a rectangular prism?

10	8	6	12
⚬	⚬	⚬	⚬

26 **What does the measuring scale show the mass of some oranges is?**

- ⚬ about 3½ kg
- ⚬ about 6 kg
- ⚬ about 5½ kg
- ⚬ about 4½ kg

27 Which one of these algorithms does NOT involve trading?

Shade one bubble

○	○	○	○
+ 380	+ 254	+ 253	+ 334
241	305	464	185
───	───	───	───

28 Casey was checking how to measure various things.

She was told one of the following was incorrect in the list below.

Which one is incorrect?

○ Use kilometres to measure the distance between cities.

○ Use litres to measure the amount of water in a bucket.

○ Use centimetres to measure the distance across a large river.

○ Use metres to measure how high a large tree is.

29 Dora is 138 cm tall.

Her sister is half Dora's height.

How tall is Dora's sister?

Write your answer in the box.

☐ cm

30 Gina measured part of her school playground.

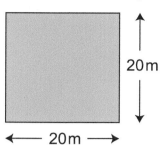

20m

20m

What is the area of the part of the playground she measured?

200 m²   20 m²   400 m²   40 m²

○   ○   ○   ○

31 Sam used a scale of 1 cm = 1 km to show the distance between his home and his school.

8 cm

home ←————————————————→ school

What is the real distance between Sam's home and his school?

ANSWER = [   ] km

32

☐☐ r ☐

3) 70

33 On the 1 cm grid below, draw a rectangle with a perimeter of 14 cm.

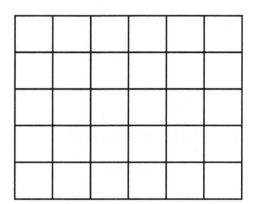

34 Use a protractor to measure the size of this angle.

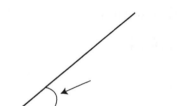

Write your answer in the box.

☐ degrees

35 This table shows how many books were borrowed from a library for a week.

Mon.	39 books
Tues.	49 books
Wed.	99 books
Thur.	51 books
Fri.	61 books
Sat.	150 books
Sun.	50 books

How many books were borrowed from the library altogether?

ANSWER = ☐

36

Bus Time Table	
First Bus	5.50 a.m.
Second Bus	6.30 a.m.
Third Bus	7.10 a.m.
Fourth Bus	

These are the times that buses pass a bus stop.

The same amount of time is between the arrival of each bus.

When will the next bus come?

8 a.m.	7.30 a.m.	7.50 a.m.	8.10 a.m.
◯	◯	◯	◯

37 A small koala has a mass of 1438 grams.

1438 grams is the same as

0.1438 kg	14.38 kg	1.438 kg	143.8 kg
◯	◯	◯	◯

38 A tap drips 50 mL every 10 minutes.

How long will it take to drip a litre of water?

◯ 50 minutes

◯ 150 minutes

◯ 100 minutes

◯ 200 minutes

39 The number that is 1000 more than 14 906 is

15 609   16 906   15 906   24 906

◯   ◯   ◯   ◯

Shade one bubble

40 A solid is made. It has one face, no edges and no corners.

What solid is it?

◯ a cylinder

◯ a sphere

◯ a cone

◯ a hemisphere

41 What is the largest number you can make by changing the order of these numbers?

| 3 | 9 | 5 | 2 |

Write your answer in the box below.

42 Ken is counting backwards by 5s.

100, 95, ☐ , ☐ , ☐ , 75

Which number should go here?

85   90   80   65

◯   ◯   ◯   ◯

43 **Which one of these solids has the least number of faces?**

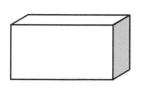 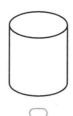 

⬭   ⬭   ⬭   ⬭

44 **What fraction of the grid is shaded?**

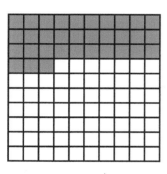

⬭ 30 out of 100

⬭ 33 out of 100

⬭ 35 out of 100

⬭ 29 out of 100

45 Colour in the date on the calendar that is exactly two weeks after 25th September.

Shade one bubble

SEPTEMBER

MON	TUES	WED	THU	FRI	SAT	SUN
		1	2	3	4	5
6	7	8	9	10	11	12
13	14	15	16	17	18	19
20	21	22	23	24	25	26
27	28	29	30			

OCTOBER

MON	TUES	WED	THU	FRI	SAT	SUN
				1	2	3
4	5	6	7	8	9	10
11	12	13	14	15	16	17
18	19	20	21	22	23	24
25	26	27	28	29	30	31

46 Danielle counted 43 seagulls at a beach. 7 flew off.

How many seagulls were still there?

35	36	37	34
◯	◯	◯	◯

47 These containers have been placed into order.

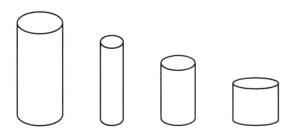

The containers are ordered according to their

width   height   volume   area

  ◯   ◯   ◯   ◯

48 Jennifer wishes to buy four items. The items have these prices.

| 90c | 40c | 70c | 60c |

Jennifer will need

◯ more than $3.00

◯ exactly $3.00

◯ less than $3.00

1 Look at this grid.

Shade one bubble

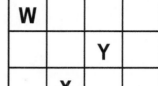

What letter is at position B2?

W   X   Y   Z

○   ○   ○   ○

---

2 **Thomas had 37 coloured pencils.**

He gave 19 to his sister.

How many coloured pencils did Thomas have left?

Write your answer in the box.

---

3 Gina has 24 cards. Jessie has twice as many cards as Gina.

How many cards does Jessie have?

58   49   47   48

○   ○   ○   ○

---

4 Sam bought an apple for 60c and a sandwich for 90c.

What change should Sam receive from $2.00?

60c   55c   50c   40c

○   ○   ○   ○

5 This graph shows the number of people voting for their favourite colour.

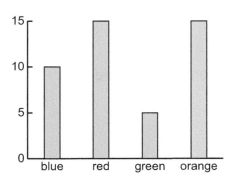

Altogether, how many people voted for their favourite colour?

45   55   35   50

⚪   ⚪   ⚪   ⚪

6 Sam's father is 185 cm tall.

185 cm is

⚪ more than 2 metres

⚪ equal to 2 metre

⚪ less than 2 metres

7 **Which one of these number sentences is NOT correct?**

⚪ 8 x 3 = 24

⚪ 7 x 3 = 21

⚪ 7 x 4 = 29

⚪ 6 x 10 = 60

8 **Circle enough of the coins below to show $2.50.**

$1   50c   50c   20c

20c   10c   5c

9 Max made this object.

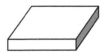

Which set of shapes did Max use tomake the above object?

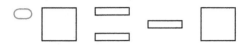

10 Ann took 64.50 seconds to run around the school playground.

This is

⚪ more than a minute

⚪ equal to a minute

⚪ less than a minute

11 Here is where some students sit in their classroom.

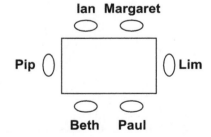

Which one of these sentences is NOT true?

⚪ Beth is next to Paul.

⚪ Lim is opposite Pip.

⚪ Lim is opposite Margaret.

⚪ Ian is opposite Beth.

12 John has 3 coins in his pocket. The coins add up to 90c.

   How many 20c coins does he have?

   [   ]

13 What is the area of this shape?

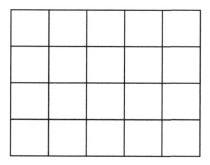

   ◯   ◯   ◯

   20 squares   24 squares   22 squares

14 Colour three quarters of this shape.

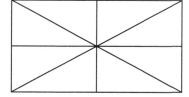

15 **Which shapes have the same perimeter?**

Shade one bubble

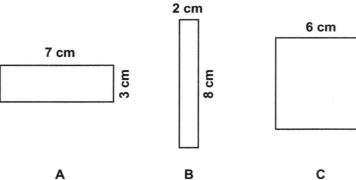

A	B	C
○	○	○
A and C	A and B	B and C

16 **Colour the octagon.**

17 Ron has collected 79 stamps. He added another 40 stamps to his collection.

How many stamps has he now?

110	120	119	118
○	○	○	○

18 Michael is at **X**.

What does Michael see when he looks in a south-east direction?

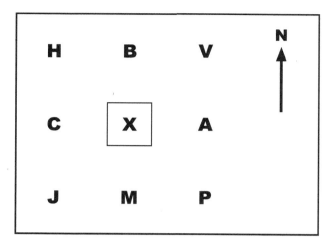

ANSWER: _____

19 There are 100 students in a library. 61 of the students are girls.

What percentage of the students are boys?

41%   29%   39%   49%

⬭   ⬭   ⬭   ⬭

20 Rita began reading a book at 8.15. She finished reading the

book in 50 minutes. **What time did she finish reading the book?**

9:15   9:00   9:10   9:05

⬭   ⬭   ⬭   ⬭

21 Sonya made 100 cards. She placed the cards into packets.

Each packet contained 9 cards.

How many cards are left over?

1   3   2   4

⬭   ⬭   ⬭   ⬭

22 Three people read the same book. They read for 10 minutes.
This tally shows how many pages they read in that time.

Names	Pages read
Tony	⫫ //
Henry	⫫ ///
Paul	⫫ ⫫

Who read the least pages?

○ Tony

○ Henry

○ Paul

23 A book costs $27. Mark has a $50 note to pay for it.

How much change should he receive when he buys the book?

Write your answer in the box.

$

24 Harry completed this graph to show the size of his friends' shoes.

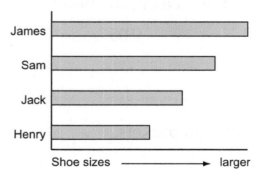

Who had the smallest shoes?

James   Sam   Jack   Henry

○   ○   ○   ○

25 Lisa used 6 straws to make a triangular pyramid frame.

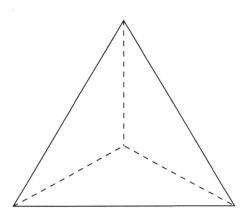

Shade one bubble

How many straws does she need to make the skeleton of

a square pyramid?

10	8	6	12
○	○	○	○

26 What does the measuring scale show the mass of some apples is?

○ about 8½ kg

○ about 6 kg

○ about 7½ kg

○ about 6½ kg

27 **Which one of these algorithms does NOT involve trading?** Shade one bubble

○	○	○	○
+ 390	+ 284	+ 253	+ 374
241	306	424	185
——	——	——	——

28 Connie was checking how to measure various things.

She was told one of the following was incorrect in the list below.

Which one is incorrect?

○ Use kilograms to measure the mass of a person.

○ Use litres to measure the amount of petrol in a car.

○ Use grams to measure the weight of a large truck.

○ Use metres to measure how high a wall is.

29 Sarah is 142 cm tall.

Her sister is half Sarah's height.

How tall is Sarah's sister?

Write your answer in the box.

☐ cm

30 Ruth measured part of her school playground.

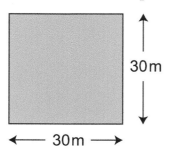

30 m

← 30 m →

Shade one bubble

What is the area of the part of the playground she measured?

600 m²   90 m²   900 m²   990 m²

◯   ◯   ◯   ◯

31 Peter used a scale of 1 cm = 1 km to show the distance between his home and his school.

11 cm

home ←————————————————→ school

What is the real distance between Peter's home and his school?

ANSWER = [   ] km

32

☐☐ r ☐
3) 80

33 On the 1 cm grid below, draw a rectangle with a perimeter of 14 cm.

Shade one bubble

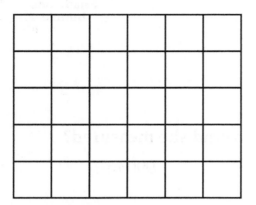

34 Use a protractor to measure the size of this angle.

Write your answer in the box.

[   ] degrees

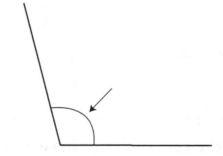

35 This table shows how many books were borrowed from a library for a week.

Mon.	30 books
Tues.	50 books
Wed.	40 books
Thur.	50 books
Fri.	60 books
Sat.	120 books
Sun.	70 books

How many books were borrowed from the library altogether?

ANSWER = [   ]

36

Bus Time Table	
First Bus	5.55 a.m.
Second Bus	6.30 a.m.
Third Bus	7.05 a.m.
Fourth Bus	

These are the times that buses pass a bus stop.

The same amount of time is between the arrival of each bus.

When will the next bus come?

7.35 a.m.   7.40 a.m.   7.45 a.m.   7.30 a.m.

○   ○   ○   ○

37 A dog has a mass of 3469 grams. **3469 grams is the same as**

0.3469 kg   34.69 kg   3.469 kg   3436.9 kg

○   ○   ○   ○

38 A tap drips 10 mL every 10 minutes.

How long will it take to drip a litre of water?

○ 10 minutes

○ 100 minutes

○ 1000 minutes

○ 10 000 minutes

39 The number that is 1000 more than 19 506 is

Shade one bubble

19 500	20 506	19 506	20 605
⬭	⬭	⬭	⬭

40 A solid shape is made. It has three faces, two edges and no corners.

What shape is it?

⬭ a cylinder

⬭ a sphere

⬭ a cone

⬭ a hemisphere

41 **What is the largest number you can make by changing the order of these numbers?**

| 4 | 7 | 0 | 8 |

Write your answer in the box below.

42 Ken is counting backwards by 3s.

100, 97, ☐ , ☐ , ☐ , 85

Which number should go here?

89	90	88	87
⬭	⬭	⬭	⬭

43 **Which one of these solids has the most number of faces?**

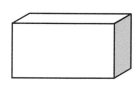  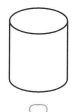 

   ◯   ◯   ◯   ◯

44 **What fraction of the grid is shaded?**

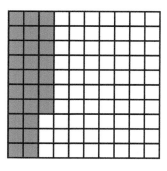

◯ 20 out of 100

◯ 27 out of 100

◯ 37 out of 100

◯ 23 out of 100

45 Colour in the date on the calendar that is exactly two weeks after 27th September.

Shade one bubble

SEPTEMBER

MON	TUES	WED	THU	FRI	SAT	SUN
		1	2	3	4	5
6	7	8	9	10	11	12
13	14	15	16	17	18	19
20	21	22	23	24	25	26
27	28	29	30			

OCTOBER

MON	TUES	WED	THU	FRI	SAT	SUN
				1	2	3
4	5	6	7	8	9	10
11	12	13	14	15	16	17
18	19	20	21	22	23	24
25	26	27	28	29	30	31

46 Danielle counted 61 seagulls at a beach. 14 flew off.

How many seagulls were still there?

45	45	47	57
○	○	○	○

47 These containers have been placed into order.

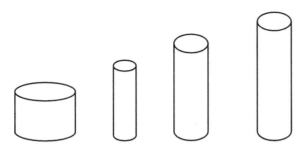

The containers are ordered according to their

width	height	volume	area
◯	◯	◯	◯

48 Jennifer wishes to buy four items. The items have these prices.

80c	70c	60c	40c

Jennifer will need

◯ more than $2.50

◯ exactly $2.50

◯ less than $2.50

1 Look at this grid.

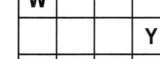
Shade one bubble

W			
			Y
X			
			Z

4
3
2
1
A   B   C   D

What letter is at position A4?

W   X   Y   Z
○   ○   ○   ○

2 Ken had 57 coloured pencils.

He gave 28 to his sister.

How many coloured pencils did Ken have left?

Write your answer in the box.

3 Pauline has 39 cards. Jessica has twice as many cards as Pauline.

How many cards does Jessica have?

68   79   77   78
○   ○   ○   ○

4 Terri bought an apple for 45c and a sandwich for 95c.

What change should Terri receive from $2.00?

60c   55c   50c   70c
○   ○   ○   ○

5   This graph shows the number of people voting for their favourite colour.

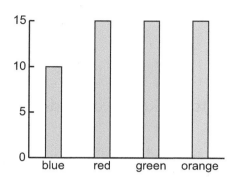

Altogether, how many people voted for their favourite colour?

45   55   35   50
◯   ◯   ◯   ◯

6   Timothy's mother is 150 cm tall.

150 cm is

◯ more than 1 ½ metres

◯ equal to 1 ½ metres

◯ less than 1 ½ metres

7   **Which one of these number sentences is NOT correct?**

◯ 9 x 4 = 36

◯ 8 x 5 = 41

◯ 9 x 5 = 45

◯ 7 x 7 = 49

8   **Circle enough of the coins below to show $2.30.**

$1   50c   50c   20c

20c   10c   10c   5c

9 Christopher made this cylinder with two ends.

Shade one bubble

Which set of shapes below Christopher use to make the cylinder?

⊖ ◯ ○ ▭

⊖ ◯ ▭

⊖ ◯ ◯ ▭

10 Anna has a choice between these buys.

Which is the cheapest buy?

⊖ 20 cents each

⊖ 3 for 50 cents

⊖ 8 for one dollar

⊖ 10 cents each

11 Two groups visited the zoo.

One group had 27 people. The other group had 29 people.

How many people were in the two groups?

Write your answer in the box.

☐

12 This is the time on Jan's watch.

```
10:25
```

This is the time on Joseph's watch.

```
11:05
```

What is the difference between the two times?

20 minutes   50 minutes   30 minutes   40 minutes
  ◯   ◯   ◯   ◯

13 What is the area of this shape?

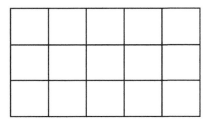

    12 squares   16 squares   15 squares
      ◯   ◯   ◯

14 Colour four eighths of this shape.

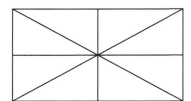

15 **Which shapes have the same perimeter?**

Shade one bubble

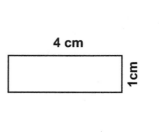
4 cm
1 cm

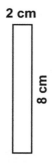
2 cm
8 cm

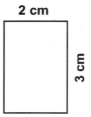
2 cm
3 cm

A   B   C

○   ○   ○

A and C   A and B   B and C

---

16 **Colour the pentagon.**

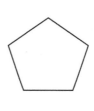 

---

17 Harry has collected 89 stamps. He added another 25 stamps to his collection.

How many stamps has he now?

113   114   115   112

○   ○   ○   ○

18 Max is at **X**.

What does Max see when he looks in a north-east direction?

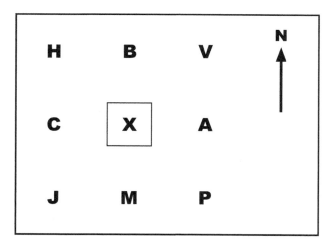

ANSWER: _____

19 There are 100 students in a library. 39 of the students are girls.

What percentage of the students are boys?

51%	62%	61%	59%
◯	◯	◯	◯

20 Ryan began reading a book at 7.50. He finished reading the book in 50 minutes. **What time did he finish reading the book?**

8:45	8:55	8:50	8:40
◯	◯	◯	◯

21 Dora made 100 cards. She placed the cards into packets.

Each packet contained 8 cards.

How many cards are left over?

1	3	2	4
◯	◯	◯	◯

22 Three people read the same book. They read for 10 minutes.

This tally shows how many pages they read in that time.

Names	Pages read
Sandra	~~HHH~~ //
Sally	~~HHH~~ ///
Sue	~~HHH~~ ~~HHH~~

How many pages did they read altogether?

23   24   25   26

○   ○   ○   ○

23 A book costs $23.50. Paul has a $50 note to pay for it.

How much change should he receive when he buys the book?

Write your answer in the box.

$ [   ]

24 Luke borrowed 6 books from the library. Stephen borrowed 7.

Peta borrowed 4. Katie borrowed 8.

How many books did they borrow altogether?

24   25   26   23

○   ○   ○   ○

25 Jean used 6 straws to make a triangular pyramid frame.

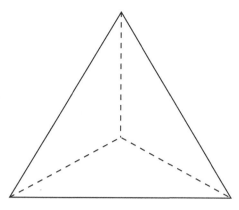

How many straws does she need to make the skeleton of a triangular prism?

7	8	9	10
⬭	⬭	⬭	⬭

26 **What does the measuring scale show the mass of some cherries is?**

⬭ about 9½ kg

⬭ about 12 kg

⬭ about 8½ kg

⬭ about 10½ kg

27 **Which one of these algorithms does NOT involve trading?**

Shade one
bubble

○   ○   ○   ○

+ 690	+ 294	+ 203	+ 394
271	308	424	585
———	———	———	———

28 Con was checking how to measure various things.

He was told one of the following was incorrect in the list below.

Which one is incorrect?

○ Use kilometres to measure the mass of a book.

○ Use litres to measure the amount of milk in a bottle.

○ Use millilitres to measure the amount of water in a glass.

○ Use centimetres to measure the length of a pen.

29 Fran is 116 cm tall.

Her sister is half Fran's height.

How tall is Fran's sister?

Write your answer in the box.

☐ cm

30 Alison measured part of her school playground.

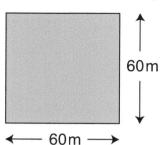

60m

← 60m →

What is the area of the part of the playground she measured?

6000 m²   3600 m²   360 m²   1200 m²

○   ○   ○   ○

31 James used a scale of 1 cm = 1 km to show the distance between his home and his school.

25½ cm

home ←⎯⎯⎯⎯⎯⎯⎯⎯⎯⎯⎯⎯⎯⎯→ school

What is the real distance between James's home and his school?

ANSWER = ⬚ km

32

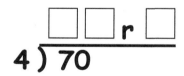

$$4\overline{)70}$$

33 On the 1 cm grid below, draw a rectangle with a perimeter of 22 cm.

Shade one bubble

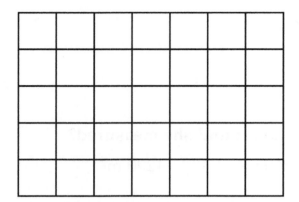

34 Use a protractor to measure the size of this angle.

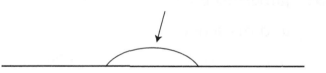

Write your answer in the box.

[ ] degrees

35 This table shows how many books were borrowed from a library for a week.

Mon.	25 books
Tues.	50 books
Wed.	25 books
Thur.	50 books
Fri.	75 books
Sat.	125 books
Sun.	75 books

How many books were borrowed from the library altogether?

ANSWER = [ ]

36

Bus Time Table	
First Bus	6.05 a.m.
Second Bus	7.10 a.m.
Third Bus	8.15 a.m.
Fourth Bus	

These are the times that buses pass a bus stop.

The same amount of time is between the arrival of each bus.

When will the next bus come?

8.20 a.m.   9.20 a.m.   9.25 a.m.   10.30 a.m.
  ○   ○   ○   ○

37 A cat has a mass of 2409 grams.

2409 grams is the same as

0.2409 kg   24.09 kg   2.409 kg   240.9 kg
  ○   ○   ○   ○

38 A tap drips 100 mL every 2 minutes.

How long will it take to drip a litre of water?

○ 5 minutes

○ 15 minutes

○ 10 minutes

○ 20 minutes

39 **The number that is 1000 less than 18 006 is**

19 006   17 006   17 060   20 006

⟞ ⟞ ⟞ ⟞ ⟞   ⟞ ⟞   ⟞ ⟞   ⟞ ⟞

Shade one bubble

40 A solid shape is made. It has two faces, one edge and no corners.

What shape is it?

⟞ a cylinder

⟞ a sphere

⟞ a cone

⟞ a hemisphere

41 **What is the largest number you can make by changing the order of these numbers?**

| 3 | 9 | 0 | 9 |

Write your answer in the box below.

42 Kerri is counting backwards by 6s.

100, 94, ☐ , ☐ , ☐ , 70

Which number should go here?

78   82   76   80

⟞   ⟞   ⟞   ⟞

43 **Which one of these solids has the least number of faces?**

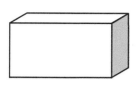   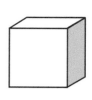

    ◯   ◯   ◯   ◯

44 **What fraction of the grid is shaded?**

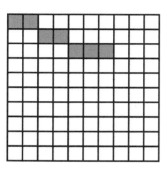

◯ 7 out of 100

◯ 93 out of 100

◯ 9 out of 100

◯ 8 out of 100

45 Colour in the date on the calendar that is exactly two weeks after 30th September.

Shade one bubble

SEPTEMBER						
MON	**TUES**	**WED**	**THU**	**FRI**	**SAT**	**SUN**
		1	2	3	4	5
6	7	8	9	10	11	12
13	14	15	16	17	18	19
20	21	22	23	24	25	26
27	28	29	30			

OCTOBER						
MON	**TUES**	**WED**	**THU**	**FRI**	**SAT**	**SUN**
				1	2	3
4	5	6	7	8	9	10
11	12	13	14	15	16	17
18	19	20	21	22	23	24
25	26	27	28	29	30	31

46 Leon counted 91 seagulls at a beach. 32 flew off.

How many seagulls were still there?

49	59	69	58
○	○	○	○

47 Jenny measured the length of each side of this shape.

Then Jenny added the lengths together.

Jenny has worked out the shape's

mass	perimeter	volume	area
⬭	⬭	⬭	⬭

48 Jackie wishes to buy four items. The items have these prices.

| 60c | 60c | 60c | 60c |

Jackie will need

⬭ more than $2.40

⬭ exactly $2.40

⬭ less than $2.40

1   Look at this grid.

4	Z			
3	W			
2	Y			
1	X			
	A	B	C	D

What letter is at position A3?

W   X   Y   Z
○   ○   ○   ○

---

2   **Kieran had 77 coloured pencils.**

He gave 48 to his sister.

How many coloured pencils did Kieran have left?

Write your answer in the box.

[   ]

---

3   Paula has 57 cards. Jessie has twice as many cards as Paula.

How many cards does Jessie have?

94   114   104   115
○   ○   ○   ○

---

4   Tess bought an apple for 39c and a sandwich for 99c.

What change should Tess receive from $2.00?

60c   55c   62c   70c
○   ○   ○   ○

5 This graph shows the number of people voting for their favourite colour.

Altogether, how many people voted for their favourite colour?

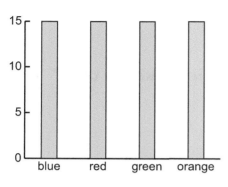

45 ⬭   55 ⬭   75 ⬭   60 ⬭

6 Terry's mother is 160 cm tall.

160 cm is

⬭ more than 1 ½ metres

⬭ equal to 1 ½ metres

⬭ less than 1 ½ metres

7 **Which one of these number sentences is NOT correct?**

⬭ 9 x 6 = 54

⬭ 11 x 5 = 50

⬭ 5 x 9 = 45

⬭ 7 x 7 = 49

8 **Circle enough of the coins below to show $5.80.**

$2	$2	$1	50c
20c	20c	10c	5c

9 Christopher made this cone.

Which set of shapes below Christopher use to make the cone?

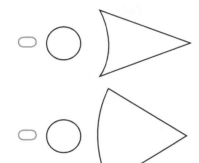

10 Alex has a choice between these buys.

Which is the cheapest buy?

○ 30 cents each

○ 2 for 50 cents

○ 5 for one dollar

○ 25 cents each

11 Two groups visited the zoo.

One group had 27 people. The other group had 35 people.

How many people were in the two groups?

Write your answer in the box.

12 This is the time on Jan's watch.

| 10:45 |

This is the time on Joseph's watch.

| 11:25 |

What is the difference between the two times?

35 minutes   50 minutes   45 minutes   40 minutes

◯   ◯   ◯   ◯

13 **What is the area of this shape?**

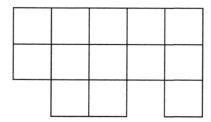

12 squares   13 squares   14 squares

◯   ◯   ◯

14 **Colour six eighths of this shape.**

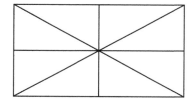

15 **Which shapes have the same perimeter?**

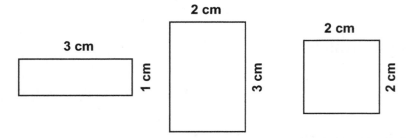

A ⭕ B ⭕ C ⭕

A and C   A and B   B and C

---

16 **Colour the parallelogram.**

---

17 Craig has collected 69 stamps. He added another 47 stamps to his collection.

How many stamps has he now?

114	115	116	117
⭕	⭕	⭕	⭕

18 Paul is at X.

What does Paul see when he looks in a north-west direction?

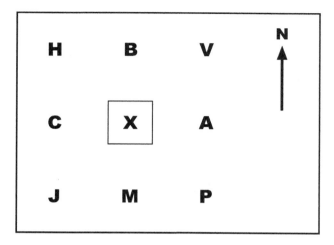

ANSWER: _____

19 There are 100 students in a library. 41 of the students are girls.

What percentage of the students are boys?

57%	62%	61%	59%
○	○	○	○

20 Jeremy began reading a book at 8.45. He finished reading the book in 65 minutes. **What time did he finish reading the book?**

9:45	9:55	9:50	9:40
○	○	○	○

21 George made 100 cards. He placed the cards into packets.

Each packet contained 7 cards.

How many cards are left over?

1	3	2	4
○	○	○	○

22 Three people read the same book. They read for 10 minutes. This tally shows how many pages they read in that time.

Shade one bubble

Names	Pages read
Sam	HHH HHH
Tim	HHH ///
Ron	HHH HHH

How many pages did they read altogether?

25   26   27   28

○   ○   ○   ○

23 A book costs $27.50. Jeff has a $50 note to pay for it.

How much change should he receive when he buys the book?

Write your answer in the box.

$ [   ]

24 Kevin borrowed 9 books from the library. Harry borrowed 8.

Sarah borrowed 7. Kylie borrowed 9.

How many books did they borrow altogether?

34   35   36   33

○   ○   ○   ○

25 Jean used 6 straws to make a triangular pyramid frame.

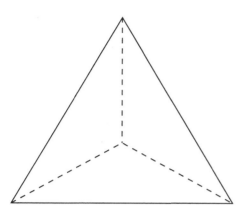

Shade one bubble

How many straws does she need to make the skeleton of a cube?

11	8	12	10
○	○	○	○

26 What does the measuring scale show the mass of some cherries to be?

○ about 2½ kg

○ about 0 kg

○ about 1½ kg

○ about ½ kg

27 Which one of these algorithms does NOT involve trading?

Shade one bubble

◯	◯	◯	◯
+ 660	+ 391	+ 478	+ 379
471	308	464	585
———	———	———	———

28 Frank was checking how to measure various things.

He was told one of the following was incorrect in the list below.

Which one is incorrect?

◯ Use kilograms to measure the mass of a bag of potatoes.

◯ Use litres to measure the amount of petrol in a container.

◯ Use grams to measure the amount of medicine in a tiny glass.

◯ Use centimetres to measure the length of a piece of string.

29 Lisa is 118 cm tall.

Her sister is half Lisa's height.

How tall is Lisa's sister?

Write your answer in the box.

☐ cm

30 Alicia measured part of her school playground.

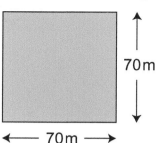

70m

← 70m →

What is the area of the part of the playground she measured?

7000 m²   490 m²   4900 m²   1400 m²

 ⬭   ⬭   ⬭   ⬭

31 James used a scale of 1 cm = 1 km to show the distance between his home and his school.

17½ cm

home ⟵─────────────────────────────⟶ school

What is the real distance between James's home and his school?

ANSWER = ☐ km

32

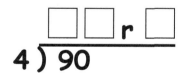

33 On the 1 cm grid below, draw a rectangle with a perimeter of 20 cm.

Shade one bubble

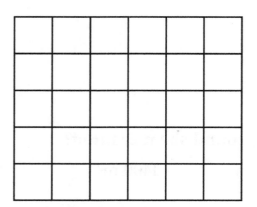

34 Use a protractor to measure the size of this angle.

Write your answer in the box.

☐ degrees

35 This table shows how many books were borrowed from a library for a week.

Mon.	25 books
Tues.	50 books
Wed.	75 books
Thur.	50 books
Fri.	75 books
Sat.	75 books
Sun.	60 books

How many books were borrowed from the library altogether?

ANSWER = ☐

36

Bus Time Table	
First Bus	6.20 a.m.
Second Bus	6.55 a.m.
Third Bus	7.30 a.m.
Fourth Bus	

These are the times that buses pass a bus stop.

The same amount of time is between the arrival of each bus.

When will the next bus come?

8.10 a.m.   8.00 a.m.   9.05 a.m.   8.05 a.m.
○   ○   ○   ○

37 A fish has a mass of 2739 grams.

2739 grams is the same as

0.2739 kg   27.39 kg   2.739 kg   273.9 kg
○   ○   ○   ○

38 A tap drips 100 mL every 5 minutes.

How long will it take to drip a litre of water?

○ 50 minutes

○ 55 minutes

○ 100 minutes

○ 60 minutes

39 The number that is 1000 less than 10 006 is

    9 006   8 006   11 006   6

    ◯   ◯   ◯   ◯

Shade one bubble

40 A solid shape is made. It has two faces, one edge and one corner.

What shape is it?

◯ a cylinder

◯ a sphere

◯ a cone

◯ a hemisphere

41 What is the largest number you can make by changing the order of these numbers?

| 5 | 9 | 8 | 3 |

Write your answer in the box below.

| |

42 Tammy is counting backwards by 7s.

100, 93, ☐ , ☐ , ☐ , 65

Which number should go here?

    78   79   77   80

    ◯   ◯   ◯   ◯

43 **Which one of these solids has the least number of edges?**

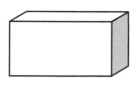   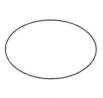

     ◯   ◯   ◯   ◯

44 **What fraction of the grid is shaded?**

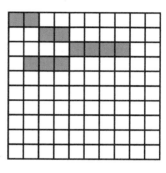

◯ 11 out of 100

◯ 21 out of 100

◯ 81 out of 100

◯ 18 out of 100

45 Colour in the date on the calendar that is exactly two weeks after 26th September.

Shade one bubble

SEPTEMBER

MON	TUES	WED	THU	FRI	SAT	SUN
		1	2	3	4	5
6	7	8	9	10	11	12
13	14	15	16	17	18	19
20	21	22	23	24	25	26
27	28	29	30			

OCTOBER

MON	TUES	WED	THU	FRI	SAT	SUN
				1	2	3
4	5	6	7	8	9	10
11	12	13	14	15	16	17
18	19	20	21	22	23	24
25	26	27	28	29	30	31

46 Wendy counted 77 seagulls at a beach. 28 flew off.

How many seagulls were still there?

49	59	39	48
○	○	○	○

47 Kerrie measured the length of each side of this shape.

Then Kerrie added the lengths together.

Shade one bubble

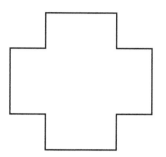

Kerrie has worked out the shape's

mass	volume	perimeter	area
⬭	⬭	⬭	⬭

48 Jean wishes to buy four items. The items have these prices.

| 70c | 70c | 70c | 70c |

Jean will need

⬭ more than $2.70

⬭ exactly $2.70

⬭ less than $2.70

1   **Look at this grid.**

Shade one bubble

4	W	Y	X	Z
3				
2				
1				
	A	B	C	D

What letter is at position D4?

W   X   Y   Z

○   ○   ○   ○

2   **Ken had 96 coloured pencils.**

He gave 48 to his sister.

How many coloured pencils did Ken have left?

Write your answer in the box.

3   Pauline has 79 cards. Jan has twice as many cards as Pauline.

How many cards does Jan have?

144   159   157   158

○   ○   ○   ○

4   Sam bought an apple for 29c and a sandwich for $1.55. What change should Sam receive from $2.00?

16c   15c   12c   17c

○   ○   ○   ○

5   This graph shows the number of people voting for their favourite colour. Altogether, how many people voted for their favourite colour?

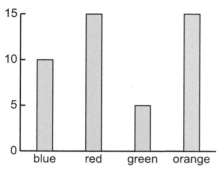

45	50	35	40
⬭	⬭	⬭	⬭

6   A tree is 395 cm high.

395 cm is

⬭ more than 3 ½ metres

⬭ equal to 3 ½ metres

⬭ less than 3 ½ metres

7   **Which one of these number sentences is NOT correct?**

⬭ 9 x 7 = 63

⬭ 7 x 8 = 57

⬭ 6 x 9 = 54

⬭ 7 x 9 = 63

8   **Circle enough of the coins below to show $5.90.**

$2	$2	$2	$1
50c	20c	10c	10c

9   A car's fuel gauge shows full when the tank has

80 litres of petrol in it.

About how many litres of petrol are shown by the

arrow in the car's fuel guage?

Shade one bubble

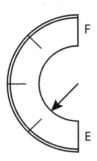

20	60	40	80
⭕	⭕	⭕	⭕

10   Alex has a choice between these buys.

Which is the cheapest buy?

- ⭕ 40 cents each
- ⭕ 2 for 70 cents
- ⭕ 4 for one dollar
- ⭕ 35 cents each

11   Two groups visited the zoo.

One group had 37 people. The other group had 49 people.

How many people were in the two groups?

Write your answer in the box.

12 This is the time on Jan's watch.

10:40

This is the time on Joseph's watch.

11:15

What is the difference between the two times?

35 minutes   50 minutes   45 minutes   40 minutes

○   ○   ○   ○

13 **What is the area of this shape?**

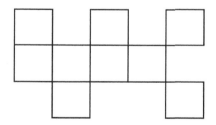

10 squares   9 squares   11 squares   8 squares

○   ○   ○   ○

14 **Colour eight eighths of this shape.**

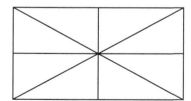

15 **37 + 6 + 7 + 20 =** ◻

Shade one bubble

The answer to this number sentence is equal to

40	50	60	70
○	○	○	○

---

16 Books are on sale 2 for $5.

Elizabeth paid $20 for her books.

How many books did Elizabeth buy?

6	8	10	12
○	○	○	○

---

17 Darren has collected 79 stamps.

He added another 38 stamps to his collection.

How many stamps has he now?

118	115	116	117
○	○	○	○

18 Chris is at **X**.

What letter does Chris see when he looks in a westerly direction?

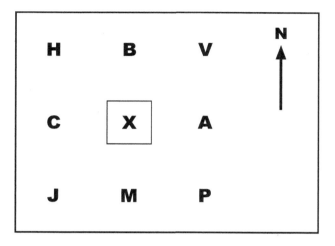

ANSWER: _____

19 There are 100 students in a library. 81 of the students are boys.

What percentage of the students are girls?

27%	17%	19%	29%
◯	◯	◯	◯

20 Jeff began reading a book at 8.05. He finished reading the book in 85 minutes. **What time did he finish reading the book?**

9:25	9:35	9:40	9:30
◯	◯	◯	◯

21 Gina made 100 cards. She placed the cards into packets.

Each packet contained 6 cards.

How many cards are left over?

1	3	2	4
◯	◯	◯	◯

22 Four stopwatch times for a race are compared.

Which stopwatch shows the fastest time?

Shade one bubble

○ 00:1:59

○ 00:1:30

○ 00:1:25

○ 00:1:49

23 A book costs $33.50. Kath has a $50 note to pay for it.

How much change should she receive when she buys the book?

Write your answer in the box.

$ ☐

24 Nancy borrowed 6 books from the library. Henry borrowed 9.

Pip borrowed 10. Kylie borrowed 10.

How many books did they borrow altogether?

34	35	36	33
○	○	○	○

25 **Which of these shapes has more than one line of symmetry?**

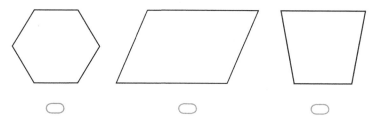

○   ○   ○

26 **What does the measuring scale show the mass of some potatoes to be?**

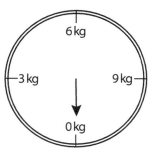

○ about 11 kg

○ about 10 kg

○ about 12 kg

○ about 13 kg

27 **Which one of these algorithms does NOT involve trading?** Shade one bubble

⚪	⚪	⚪	⚪
+ 320	+ 390	+ 485	+ 699
471	478	464	585
——	——	——	——

28 Richard was checking how to measure various things.

He was told one of the following was incorrect in the list below.

Which one is incorrect?

⚪ Use grams to measure the volume of a glass of water.

⚪ Use millilitres to measure the capacity of a small container.

⚪ Use litres to measure the amount of petrol in a petrol tank.

⚪ Use centimetres to measure the length of a shoe.

29 Carl is 122 cm tall.

His sister is half Carl's height.

How tall is Carl's sister?

Write your answer in the box.

☐ cm

30 Alex measured part of her school playground.

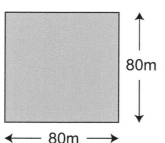

80m

← 80m →

What is the area of the part of the playground she measured?

640 m²   320 m²   1600 m²   6400 m²

○   ○   ○   ○

31 Ruth used a scale of 1 cm = 1 km to show the distance between her home

and her school.

7½ cm

home ←――――――――――――――――→ school

What is the real distance between Ruth's home and her school?

ANSWER = ☐ km

32

$$\begin{array}{r} \square\,\square\,r\,\square \\ 7\,\overline{)\,90} \end{array}$$

33 On the 1 cm grid below, draw a rectangle with a perimeter of 12 cm.

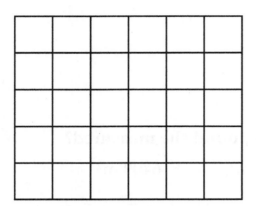

34 Use a protractor to measure the size of this angle.

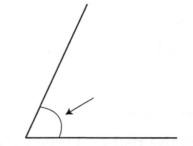

Write your answer in the box.

☐ degrees

35 This table shows how many plants were bought from a nursery in a week.

Mon.	30 books
Tues.	40 books
Wed.	50 books
Thur.	60 books
Fri.	70 books
Sat.	80 books
Sun.	90 books

How many books were borrowed from the library altogether?

ANSWER = ☐

36

Bus Time Table	
First Bus	6.55 a.m.
Second Bus	7.45 a.m.
Third Bus	8.35 a.m.
Fourth Bus	

These are the times that buses pass a bus stop.

The same amount of time is between the arrival of each bus.

When will the next bus come?

  9.30 a.m.   9.20 a.m.   9.25 a.m.   9.35 a.m.

    ◯   ◯   ◯   ◯

37   A chair has a mass of 4039 grams.

4039 grams is the same as

  0.4039 kg   40.39 kg   4.039 kg   403.9 kg

    ◯   ◯   ◯   ◯

38   A tap drips 100 mL every 15 minutes.

How long will it take to drip a litre of water?

◯   15 minutes

◯   150 minutes

◯   125 minutes

◯   200 minutes

39 The number that is 1000 less than 20 105 is

9 105	8 105	19 105	5
◯	◯	◯	◯

Shade one bubble

40 A solid is made. It has four faces, six edges and four corners.

What solid is it?

- ◯ a sphere
- ◯ a triangular prism
- ◯ a cube
- ◯ a triangular pyramid

41 **What is the largest number you can make by changing the order of these numbers?**

| 7 | 1 | 6 | 9 |

Write your answer in the box below.

42 Tammy is counting backwards by 9s.

100, 91, ☐ , ☐ , ☐ , 55

Which number should go here?

74	73	64	72
◯	◯	◯	◯

43 Anne had a 500 mL carton of juice.

She drank half of the juice.

How much juice did Anne drink?

○ one litre

○ half a litre

○ a quarter of a litre

44 What fraction of the grid is shaded?

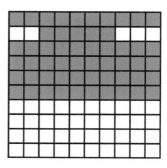

○ 55 out of 100

○ 65 out of 100

○ 45 out of 100

○ 35 out of 100

45 **Colour in the date on the calendar that is exactly two weeks after 20th September.**

Shade one bubble

SEPTEMBER

MON	TUES	WED	THU	FRI	SAT	SUN
		1	2	3	4	5
6	7	8	9	10	11	12
13	14	15	16	17	18	19
20	21	22	23	24	25	26
27	28	29	30			

OCTOBER

MON	TUES	WED	THU	FRI	SAT	SUN
				1	2	3
4	5	6	7	8	9	10
11	12	13	14	15	16	17
18	19	20	21	22	23	24
25	26	27	28	29	30	31

46 Kathleen counted 84 seagulls at a beach. 35 flew off.

How many seagulls were still there?

49	59	39	48
○	○	○	○

47 A book has 600 pages. Nicholas has read 379 pages.

How many more pages has Nicholas left to read before he has finished the book?

231	331	221	222
⟵◯⟶	⟵◯⟶	⟵◯⟶	⟵◯⟶

48 Jennie wishes to buy four items. The items have these prices.

90c	70c	90c	70c

Jennie will need

◯ more than $3.00

◯ exactly $3.00

◯ less than $3.00

1 Look at this grid.

Shade one bubble

```
4
3        Z
2     Y  W
1        X
   A  B  C  D
```

What letter is at position C2?

W	X	Y	Z
⬭	⬭	⬭	⬭

2 **Tim had 106 coloured pencils.**

He gave 39 to his sister.

How many coloured pencils did Tim have left?

Write your answer in the box.

☐

3 Paula has 58 cards. Janice has twice as many cards as Paula.

How many cards does Janice have?

114	115	117	116
⬭	⬭	⬭	⬭

4 Sonny bought an apple for 45c and a sandwich for $1.35.

What change should Sam receive from $2.00?

19c	20c	21c	25c
⬭	⬭	⬭	⬭

5   This graph shows the number of people voting for their favourite colour.

Altogether, how many people voted for their favourite colour?

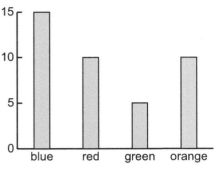

45   50   35   40

⬭   ⬭   ⬭   ⬭

6   A tree is 650 cm high.

650 cm is

⬭ more than 6 ½ metres

⬭ equal to 6 ½ metres

⬭ less than 6 ½ metres

7   **Which one of these number sentences is NOT correct?**

⬭ 9 x 6 = 54

⬭ 8 x 7 = 56

⬭ 6 x 8 = 48

⬭ 8 x 9 = 63

8   **Circle enough of the coins below to show $3.70.**

$2	$2	$2	$1
50c	20c	10c	5c

9   A car's fuel gauge shows full when the tank has

80 litres of petrol in it.

About how many litres of petrol are shown by the

arrow in the car's fuel guage?

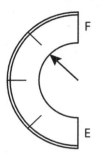

20	60	40	80
⬭	⬭	⬭	⬭

10   Alison has a choice between these buys.

Which is the cheapest buy?

⬭ 30 cents each

⬭ 2 for 60 cents

⬭ 4 for one dollar

⬭ 29 cents each

11   Two groups visited the zoo.

One group had 38 people. The other group had 29 people.

How many people were in the two groups?

Write your answer in the box.

12 This is the time on John's watch.

| 12:20 |

This is the time on Joe's watch.

| 1:15 |

What is the difference between the two times?

65 minutes   60 minutes   55 minutes   50 minutes
⬭   ⬭   ⬭   ⬭

13 **What is the area of this shape?**

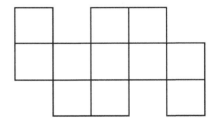

10 squares   9 squares   11 squares   8 squares
⬭   ⬭   ⬭   ⬭

14 **Colour three eighths of this shape.**

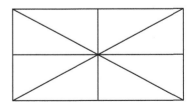

15 **27 + 9 + 7 + 30 =** [ ]

Shade one bubble

The answer to this number sentence is equal to

75	72	74	73
◯	◯	◯	◯

16 Books are on sale 2 for $3.

Elena paid $30 for her books.

How many books did Elena buy?

18	22	20	21
◯	◯	◯	◯

17 Isobel has collected 89 stamps.

She added another 36 stamps to her collection.

How many stamps has she now?

128	125	126	127
◯	◯	◯	◯

18 Max is at **X**.

What letter does Max see when he looks in a south-westerly direction?

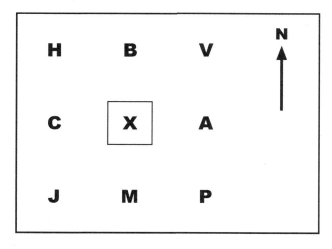

ANSWER: _____

19 There are 100 students in a library. 49 of the students are boys.

What percentage of the students are girls?

51%	52%	50%	49%
⚬	⚬	⚬	⚬

20 Jenny began reading a book at 8.25. She finished reading the book in 75 minutes. **What time did she finish reading the book?**

9:25	9:35	9:40	9:30
⚬	⚬	⚬	⚬

21 Tina made 100 cards. She placed the cards into packets.

Each packet contained 4 cards.

How many cards are left over?

1	3	2	0
⚬	⚬	⚬	⚬

22 Four stopwatch times for a race are compared.

Which stopwatch shows the fastest time?

Shade one
bubble

○ | 00:0:19 |

○ | 00:0:20 |

○ | 00:0:21 |

○ | 00:0:18 |

23 A book costs $29.50. William has a $50 note to pay for it.

How much change should he receive when he buys the book?

Write your answer in the box.

$ [   ]

24 Jean borrowed 9 books from the library. Harry borrowed 10.

Peter borrowed 9. Kelly borrowed 7.

How many books did they borrow altogether?

34	35	36	33
○	○	○	○

25 **Which of these shapes has more than one line of symmetry?**

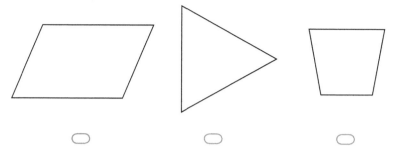

○   ○   ○

26 A box is half full of oranges.

All oranges are the same size.

After another 25 oranges are added to the box, the box is

three quarters full.

How many oranges will the box hold when it is full?

25	100	75	50
○	○	○	○

27 **Which one of these algorithms does NOT involve trading?**

+ 329	+ 390	+ 479	+ 689
671	408	464	586
────	────	────	────
○	○	○	○

28 A spider has 8 legs.

Peta wishes to draw 4 spiders.

How many legs will Peta need to draw altogether?

28	30	32	36
○	○	○	○

29 Greta is 132 cm tall.

His sister is half Greta's height.

How tall is Greta's sister?

Write your answer in the box.

☐ cm

30 Alan measured part of her school playground.

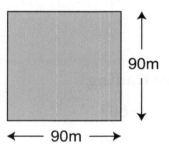

What is the area of the part of the playground she measured?

810 m²	900 m²	1800 m²	8100 m²
○	○	○	○

31 Rene used a scale of 1 cm = 1 km to show the distance between her home and her school.

1¾ cm

home ←————————————————————→ school

What is the real distance between Rene's home and her school?

ANSWER = ▢ km

32

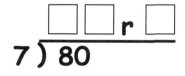

33

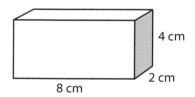

This container is 8 cm long, 2cm wide and 4cm deep.

What is the volume of water in the container when it is half full?

30 cm³   32 m³   64 m³   34 m³

  ◯   ◯   ◯   ◯

34 Which rectangle would have a perimeter of 18cm
and an area of 20cm²?

Shade one
bubble

○ a rectangle of 6 cm × 2 cm

○ a rectangle of 5 cm × 4 cm

○ a rectangle of 5 cm × 3 cm

○ a rectangle of 4 cm × 4 cm

35 Karen walked around a field three times.

The first time took 5 minutes.

The other walks took 1 minute longer than the walk before.

How long did 3 walks take?

| | minutes

36

Bus Time Table	
First Bus	6.45 a.m.
Second Bus	7.40 a.m.
Third Bus	8.35 a.m.
Fourth Bus	

These are the times that buses pass a bus stop.

The same amount of time is between the arrival of each bus.

When will the next bus come?

9.30 a.m.   9.20 a.m.   9.25 a.m.   9.35 a.m.

○   ○   ○   ○

37 A plant has a mass of 7045 grams.

7045 grams is the same as

0.7045 kg	70.45 kg	7.045 kg	704.5 kg
⬭	⬭	⬭	⬭

38 A tap drips 100 mL every 1½ minutes.

How long will it take to drip a litre of water?

- ⬭ 5 minutes
- ⬭ 15 minutes
- ⬭ 18 minutes
- ⬭ 20 minutes

39 The number that is 100 less than 1105 is

905	1105	1205	1005
⬭	⬭	⬭	⬭

40 A wall is 8 metres long.

This is the same as

- ⬭ 8 cm
- ⬭ 800 cm
- ⬭ 80 cm
- ⬭ 8000 cm

41 **What is the smallest number you can make by changing the order of these numbers?**

| 5 | 1 | 6 | 3 |

Shade one bubble

Write your answer in the box below.

42 Thomas is counting backwards by 8s.

105, 97, ☐ , ☐ , ☐ , 65

Which number should go here?

| 74 | 73 | 64 | 72 |
| ○ | ○ | ○ | ○ |

43 Lisa had a 1000 mL carton of juice.

She drank half of the juice.

How much juice did Lisa drink?

○ one litre

○ half a litre

○ a quarter of a litre

44 **What fraction of the grid is shaded?**

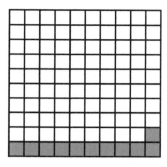

○ 100 out of 100

○ 11 out of 100

○ 99 out of 100

○ 1 out of 100

45 **Colour in the date on the calendar that is exactly three weeks**
before 10th October.

SEPTEMBER						
MON	TUES	WED	THU	FRI	SAT	SUN
		1	2	3	4	5
6	7	8	9	10	11	12
13	14	15	16	17	18	19
20	21	22	23	24	25	26
27	28	29	30			

OCTOBER						
MON	TUES	WED	THU	FRI	SAT	SUN
				1	2	3
4	5	6	7	8	9	10
11	12	13	14	15	16	17
18	19	20	21	22	23	24
25	26	27	28	29	30	31

46 Kath counted 103 seagulls at a beach. 39 flew off.

How many seagulls were still there?

63	66	64	65
○	○	○	○

47 A book has 250 pages. Nicholas has read 179 pages.

How many more pages has Nicholas left to read before he has finished the book?

61	81	71	82
○	○	○	○

48 George wishes to buy four items. The items have these prices.

85c	75c	95c	75c

George will need

○ more than $3.50

○ exactly $3.50

○ less than $3.50

1 Look at this grid.

Shade one bubble

```
4 | Y |   |   | Z |
3 |   |   |   |   |
2 |   |   |   |   |
1 | W |   |   | X |
    A   B   C   D
```

What position is X in?

A1   A4   D4   D1
○   ○   ○   ○

2 **Tom had 102 coloured pencils.**

He gave 58 to his sister.

How many coloured pencils did Tom have left?

Write your answer in the box.

☐

3 Martha has 67 cards. Jan has twice as many cards as Martha.

How many cards does Jan have?

134   135   144   133
○   ○   ○   ○

4 Dad bought an apple for 25c and a sandwich for $1.65.

What change should Dad receive from $2.00?

9c   20c   10c   11c
○   ○   ○   ○

5 This graph shows the number of people voting for their favourite colour.

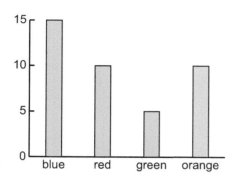

What is the difference between the colour with the most votes and the colour with the least votes?

5 votes	0 votes	10 votes	15 votes
⬭	⬭	⬭	⬭

6 A tree is 1050 cm high.

1050 cm is

- ⬭ more than 10 ½ metres
- ⬭ equal to 10 ½ metres
- ⬭ less than 10 ½ metres

7 **Which one of these number sentences is NOT correct?**

- ⬭ 7 x 6 = 42
- ⬭ 9 x 7 = 63
- ⬭ 7 x 8 = 57
- ⬭ 9 x 9 = 81

8 **Circle enough of the coins below to show $3.85.**

$2	$2	$1	50c
20c	20c	10c	5c

9   A car's fuel gauge shows full when the tank has

60 litres of petrol in it.

About how many litres of petrol are shown by the

arrow in the car's fuel guage?

Shade one
bubble

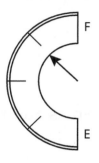

40	35	45	50
⬭	⬭	⬭	⬭

10 Barry has a choice between these buys.

Which is the cheapest buy?

◯ 40 cents each

◯ 2 for 70 cents

◯ 3 for one dollar

◯ 30 cents each

11 Two groups visited the zoo.

One group had 77 people. The other group had 66 people.

How many people were in the two groups?

Write your answer in the box.

12 This is the time on John's watch.

| 1:10 |

This is the time on Joe's watch.

| 2:05 |

What is the difference between the two times?

65 minutes   60 minutes   55 minutes   50 minutes
   ◯   ◯   ◯   ◯

13 What is the area of this shape?

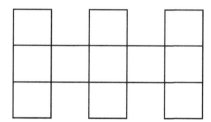

10 squares   9 squares   11 squares   8 squares
   ◯   ◯   ◯   ◯

14 Colour five eighths of this shape.

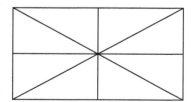

15 36 + 11 + 19 + 24 = ☐

The answer to this number sentence is equal to

85	80	100	90
⬭	⬭	⬭	⬭

16 Books are on sale 2 for $5.

Elizaeth paid $25 for her books.

How many books did Elizabeth buy?

20	5	10	15
⬭	⬭	⬭	⬭

17 Ian has collected 96 stamps.

He added another 59 stamps to his collection.

How many stamps has he now?

156	150	155	160
⬭	⬭	⬭	⬭

18 In a movie theatre are 340 people.

250 are children.

How many are not children?

Write your answer in the box.

[ ]

19 There are 100 students in a library. 57 of the students are boys.

What percentage of the students are girls?

45%   43%   44%   53%

○   ○   ○   ○

20 Jack began reading a book at 12.25. She finished reading the book in 75 minutes. **What time did he finish reading the book?**

1:35   2:40   1:40   1:30

○   ○   ○   ○

21 Harry made 110 cards. He placed the cards into packets.

Each packet contained 6 cards.

How many cards are left over?

1   3   2   0

○   ○   ○   ○

22 Four stopwatch times for a race are compared.

Which stopwatch shows the fastest time?

Shade one bubble

○ 00:2:49

○ 00:2:50

○ 00:2:37

○ 00:2:28

23 A book costs $26.50. William has a $50 note to pay for it.

How much change should he receive when he buys the book?

Write your answer in the box.

$ [ ]

24 Jan borrowed 11 books from the library. Mark borrowed 12.

Peter borrowed 9. Kim borrowed 10.

How many books did they borrow altogether?

41	40	42	43
○	○	○	○

25 The cost of 3 books is $20. Two of the books cost $6.50 each.

How much does the third book cost?

$8	$7	$8.50	$6.50
⬭	⬭	⬭	⬭

26 A box is half full of oranges.

All oranges are the same size.

After another 50 oranges are added to the box, the box is

three quarters full.

How many oranges will the box hold when it is full?

50	100	200	150
⬭	⬭	⬭	⬭

27 Which one of these algorithms does NOT involve trading?

+ 307	+ 890	+ 489	+ 687
671	408	865	596
⬭	⬭	⬭	⬭

Shade one bubble

28 A spider has 8 legs.

Grahame wishes to draw 7 spiders.

How many legs will Grahame need to draw altogether?

58	60	56	57
⬭	⬭	⬭	⬭

29 Vana is 145 cm tall.

Her sister is half Vana's height.

How tall is Vana's sister?

Write your answer in the box.

☐ cm

30 Alice measured part of her school playground.

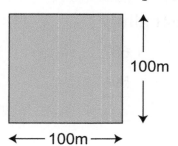
100m

←— 100m —→

What is the area of the part of the playground she measured?

400 m²	10 000 m²	100 m²	200 m²
⬭	⬭	⬭	⬭

31 David used a scale of 1 cm = 1 km to show the distance between his home and his school.

15.5 cm

home ⟵━━━━━━━━━━━━━━━━━━⟶ school

What is the real distance between David's home and his school?

ANSWER = ☐ km

32

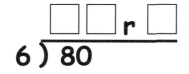

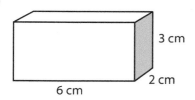

33

This container is 6 cm long, 2cm wide and 3cm deep.

What is the volume of water in the container when it is half full?

12 cm³	14 m³	18 m³	16 m³
⬭	⬭	⬭	⬭

34 Which rectangle would have a perimeter of 18 cm and an area of 18 cm²?

Shade one bubble

⭕ a rectangle of 6 cm × 2 cm

⭕ a rectangle of 5 cm × 3 cm

⭕ a rectangle of 6 cm × 3 cm

⭕ a rectangle of 4 cm × 4 cm

35 Ken walked around a field three times.

The first time took 7 minutes.

The other walks took 1 minute longer than the walk before.

How long did 3 walks take?

[   ] minutes

36

Bus Time Table	
First Bus	6.05 a.m.
Second Bus	7.10 a.m.
Third Bus	8.15 a.m.
Fourth Bus	[ ]

These are the times that buses pass a bus stop.

The same amount of time is between the arrival of each bus.

When will the next bus come?

9.20 a.m.   9.30 a.m.   9.15 a.m.   9.25 a.m.

37 An animal has a mass of 9055 grams.

9055 grams is the same as

0.9055 kg	90.55 kg	9.055 kg	905.5 kg
⬭	⬭	⬭	⬭

38 A tap drips 100 mL every 2½ minutes.

How long will it take to drip a litre of water?

⬭ 35 minutes

⬭ 25.5 minutes

⬭ 25 minutes

⬭ 20 minutes

39 The number that is 100 less than 1005 is

905	1005	950	1000
⬭	⬭	⬭	⬭

40 A wall is 7½ metres long.

This is the same as

⬭ 7½ cm

⬭ 700 cm

⬭ 750 cm

⬭ 7500 cm

41 What is the smallest number you can make by changing the order of these numbers?

Shade one bubble

| 9 | 8 | 6 | 7 |

Write your answer in the box below.

42 Thomas is counting backwards by 7s.

104, 97, ☐ , ☐ , ☐ , 69

Which number should go here?

77   75   66   76
◯   ◯   ◯   ◯

43 Lim had a 750 mL carton of juice.

She drank half of the juice.

How much juice did Lim drink?

◯ 365 mL

◯ 380 mL

◯ 375 mL

44 **What fraction of the grid is shaded?**

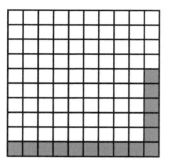

⭘ 12 out of 100

⭘ 14 out of 100

⭘ 15 out of 100

⭘ 13 out of 100

45 **Colour in the date on the calendar that is exactly three weeks before 11th October.**

SEPTEMBER						
MON	TUES	WED	THU	FRI	SAT	SUN
		1	2	3	4	5
6	7	8	9	10	11	12
13	14	15	16	17	18	19
20	21	22	23	24	25	26
27	28	29	30			

OCTOBER						
MON	TUES	WED	THU	FRI	SAT	SUN
				1	2	3
4	5	6	7	8	9	10
11	12	13	14	15	16	17
18	19	20	21	22	23	24
25	26	27	28	29	30	31

46 Kath counted 110 seagulls at a beach. 55 flew off.

How many seagulls were still there?

Shade one bubble

65	66	55	56
◯	◯	◯	◯

47 A book has 250 pages. Nicholas has read 187 pages.

How many more pages has Nicholas left to read before he has finished the book?

53	65	64	63
◯	◯	◯	◯

48 Darryl wishes to buy four items. The items have these prices.

95c	95c	95c	95c

Darryl will need

◯ more than $3.95

◯ exactly $3.95

◯ less than $3.95

Shade one bubble

1 Look at this grid.

4	Y			
3		W		
2			Z	
1				X
	A	B	C	D

What position is Z in?

C3   C2   C4   A2
◯   ◯   ◯   ◯

2 **Tim had 107 coloured pencils.**

He gave 68 to his sister.

How many coloured pencils did Tim have left?

Write your answer in the box.

☐

3 Geoff has 99 cards. Sam has twice as many cards as Geoff.

How many cards does Sam have?

200   199   197   198
◯   ◯   ◯   ◯

4 Mum bought an apple for 39c and a sandwich for $1.56.

What change should Mum receive from $2.00?

15c   10c   5c   6c
◯   ◯   ◯   ◯

5   This graph shows the number of people voting for their favourite colour.

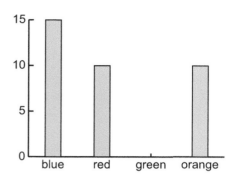

What is the difference between the colour with the most votes and the colour with the least votes?

5 votes   0 votes   10 votes   15 votes
  ○   ○   ○   ○

6   A tree is 1549 cm high.

1549 cm is

○ more than 15 ½ metres

○ equal to 15 ½ metres

○ less than 15 ½ metres

7   **Which one of these number sentences is NOT correct?**

○ 7 x 6 = 43

○ 9 x 8 = 72

○ 7 x 8 = 56

○ 6 x 9 = 54

8   **What is the answer to this number sentence?**

9 + 15 + 25 + 8 = ☐

9   A car's fuel gauge shows full when the tank has
60 litres of petrol in it.

**About how many litres of petrol are shown by the
arrow in the car's fuel guage?**

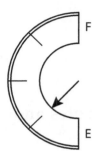

20	5	15	25
○	○	○	○

10   Barry has a choice between these buys.

Which is the cheapest buy?

○ 50 cents each

○ 2 for 90 cents

○ 2 for one dollar

○ 49 cents each

11   Two groups visited the zoo.

One group had 97 people. The other group had 96 people.

How many people were in the two groups?

Write your answer in the box.

[   ]

12 This is the time on James's watch.

| 1:59 |

This is the time on Joe's watch.

| 2:05 |

What is the difference between the two times?

5 minutes   4 minutes   7 minutes   6 minutes
   ○   ○   ○   ○

13 **What is the area of this shape?**

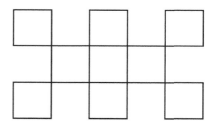

10 squares   9 squares   11 squares   8 squares
   ○   ○   ○   ○

14 **Colour seven eighths of this shape.**

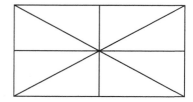

15 **29 + 11 + 29 + 11 =** [   ]

Shade one bubble

The answer to this number sentence is equal to

75	80	40	70
◯	◯	◯	◯

16 Books are on sale 2 for $7.

Elena paid $35 for her books.

How many books did Elena buy?

20	5	10	15
◯	◯	◯	◯

17 Rick has collected 99 stamps.

He added another 69 stamps to his collection.

How many stamps has he now?

167	170	168	166
◯	◯	◯	◯

18   In a movie theatre are 300 people.

120 are children.

How many are not children?

Write your answer in the box.

---

19   There are 100 students in a library. 17 of the students are boys.

What percentage of the students are girls?

73%	83%	84%	82%
◯	◯	◯	◯

---

20   John began reading a book at 9.25. He finished reading the

book in 90 minutes. **What time did he finish reading the book?**

10:55	10:15	10:50	10:45
◯	◯	◯	◯

---

21   Henry made 150 cards. He placed the cards into packets.

Each packet contained 7 cards.

How many cards are left over?

1	3	2	0
◯	◯	◯	◯

22 Four stopwatch times for a race are compared.

Which stopwatch shows the fastest time?

Shade one bubble

○ | 00:2:09 |

○ | 00:2:19 |

○ | 00:2:10 |

○ | 00:2:90 |

23 A book costs $21.50. Adam has a $50 note to pay for it.

How much change should he receive when he buys the book?

Write your answer in the box.

$ |_____|

24 Tess borrowed 9 books from the library. Michael borrowed 7.

Peter borrowed 11. Paul borrowed 8.

How many books did they borrow altogether?

35   34   36   33

○   ○   ○   ○

25 The cost of 3 books is $15. Two of the books cost $4.50 each.

How much does the third book cost?

$5.50 $6.50 $5.90 $6.00

◯   ◯   ◯   ◯

26 A box is half full of plums.

All plums are the same size.

After another 75 oranges are added to the box, the box is three quarters full.

How many oranges will the box hold when it is full?

200   400   250   300

◯   ◯   ◯   ◯

27 **Which one of these algorithms does NOT involve trading?**

```
  + 407        + 490        + 498        + 587
    674          408          865          576
    ───          ───          ───          ───

    ───          ───          ───          ───
```

◯   ◯   ◯   ◯

28 A spider has 8 legs.

Georgia wishes to draw 9 spiders.

How many legs will Georgia need to draw altogether?

78	70	72	73
⭘	⭘	⭘	⭘

29 Alana is 150 cm tall.

Her sister is half Alana's height.

How tall is Alana's sister?

Write your answer in the box.

☐ cm

30 Alice measured part of her school playground.

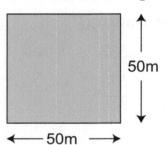

What is the area of the part of the playground she measured?

500 m²	25 000 m²	2500 m²	2000 m²
⭘	⭘	⭘	⭘

31 Daniel used a scale of 1 cm = 1 km to show the distance between his home and his school.

10.5 cm

home ⟵――――――――――――――――――――⟶ school

What is the real distance between Daniel's home and his school?

ANSWER = [＿＿＿] km

32

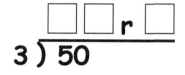

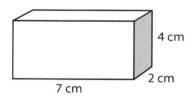

33

This container is 7 cm long, 2cm wide and 4cm deep.

What is the volume of water in the container when it is half full?

22 cm³   24 m³   26 m³   28 m³

○   ○   ○   ○

Year 5 Numeracy
NAPLAN*-Format Practice Tests

34 Which rectangle would have a perimeter of 20 cm
and an area of 24 cm²?

Shade one bubble

○ a rectangle of 6 cm × 3 cm

○ a rectangle of 5 cm × 3 cm

○ a rectangle of 6 cm × 4 cm

○ a rectangle of 7 cm × 4 cm

35 Ken walked around a field three times.

The first time took 8 minutes.

The other walks took ½ minute longer than the walk before.

How long did 3 walks take?

| | minutes

36

Bus Time Table	
First Bus	6.10 a.m.
Second Bus	7.20 a.m.
Third Bus	8.30 a.m.
Fourth Bus	

These are the times that buses pass a bus stop.

The same amount of time is between the arrival of each bus.

When will the next bus come?

9.20 a.m.   9.30 a.m.   9.35 a.m.   9.40 a.m.

37 An animal has a mass of 5555 grams.

5555 grams is the same as

0.5555 kg	55.55 kg	5.555 kg	555.5 kg
⬭	⬭	⬭	⬭

38 A tap drips 100 mL every 3½ minutes.

How long will it take to drip a litre of water?

- ⬭ 35 minutes
- ⬭ 25.5 minutes
- ⬭ 36 minutes
- ⬭ 40 minutes

39 The number that is 50 less than 1005 is

945	955	950	905
⬭	⬭	⬭	⬭

40 A wall is 5½ metres long.

This is the same as

- ⬭ 50½ cm
- ⬭ 500½ cm
- ⬭ 550 cm
- ⬭ 5500 cm

41 **What is the smallest number you can make by changing the order of these numbers?**

| 5 | 0 | 9 | 7 |

Write your answer in the box below.

| |

42 Paul is counting backwards by 8s.

103, 95, ☐ , ☐ , ☐ , 63

Which number should go here?

79   78   77   80
○   ○   ○   ○

43 Lauren had a 350 mL carton of juice.

She drank half of the juice.

How much juice did Lim drink?

○ 175 mL

○ 170 mL

○ 180 mL

44 **What fraction of the grid is shaded?**

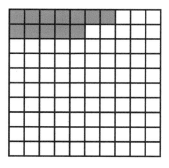

- ⬭ 15 out of 100
- ⬭ 18 out of 100
- ⬭ 12 out of 100
- ⬭ 19 out of 100

45 **Colour in the date on the calendar that is exactly three weeks before 1st October.**

SEPTEMBER						
MON	TUES	WED	THU	FRI	SAT	SUN
		1	2	3	4	5
6	7	8	9	10	11	12
13	14	15	16	17	18	19
20	21	22	23	24	25	26
27	28	29	30			

OCTOBER						
MON	TUES	WED	THU	FRI	SAT	SUN
				1	2	3
4	5	6	7	8	9	10
11	12	13	14	15	16	17
18	19	20	21	22	23	24
25	26	27	28	29	30	31

46 Robert counted 150 seagulls at a beach. 59 flew off.

How many seagulls were still there?

91   92   93   81

◯   ◯   ◯   ◯

47 A book has 250 pages. Robyn has read 119 pages.

How many more pages has Robyn left to read before she has finished the book?

130   129   131   132

◯   ◯   ◯   ◯

48 Darren wishes to buy four items. The items have these prices.

| 87c | 13c | 83c | 17c |

Darren will need

◯ more than $2.00

◯ exactly $2.00

◯ less than $2.00

1 Look at this grid.

Shade one bubble

4	Y			
3	W			
2				Z
1				X
	A	B	C	D

What position is Y in?

A3   D1   A4   D2

○   ○   ○   ○

2 Timothy had 109 coloured pencils.

He gave 79 to his sister.

How many coloured pencils did Timothy have left?

Write your answer in the box.

3 Grant has 89 cards. Simon has twice as many cards as Grant.

How many cards does Simon have?

280   179   177   178

○   ○   ○   ○

4 Mum bought an apple for 19c and a sandwich for $1.45.

What change should Mum receive from $2.00?

35c   38c   36c   37c

○   ○   ○   ○

5   A clock looks like this.

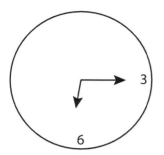

Which one of the times below is the same time as the clock above?

3:15	9:30	6:30	6:15
○	○	○	○

6   A tree is 2500 cm high.

2500 cm is

○ more than 25 metres

○ equal to 25 metres

○ less than 25 metres

7   **Which one of these number sentences is NOT correct?**

○ 8 x 6 = 48

○ 10 x 8 = 80

○ 7 x 8 = 56

○ 8 x 9 = 74

8   **What is the answer to this number sentence?**

50 + 30 + 40 + 80 = ☐

9   A car's fuel gauge shows full when the tank has
48 litres of petrol in it.

**About how many litres of petrol are shown by the
arrow in the car's fuel guage?**

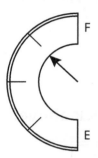

24	30	36	45
⬭	⬭	⬭	⬭

10   Brian has a choice between these buys.

Which is the cheapest buy?

⬭ 35 cents each

⬭ 3 for 90 cents

⬭ 5 for one dollar

⬭ 21 cents each

11   Two groups visited the zoo.

One group had 39 people. The other group had 79 people.

How many people were in the two groups?

Write your answer in the box.

12   This is the time on James's watch.

12:59

This is the time on Joe's watch.

1:55

What is the difference between the two times?

50 minutes   56 minutes   57 minutes   61 minutes

    ⬭   ⬭   ⬭   ⬭

13   **What is the area of this shape?**

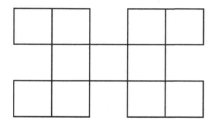

10 squares   9 squares   11 squares   8 squares

    ⬭   ⬭   ⬭   ⬭

14   **Colour one quarter of this shape.**

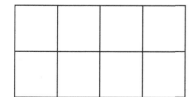

15 **79 + 21 + 79 + 21 =** ☐

Shade one bubble

The answer to this number sentence is equal to

210	190	205	200
⚪	⚪	⚪	⚪

16 Books are on sale 2 for $11.

Eva paid $55 for her books.

How many books did Eva buy?

15	10	12	9
⚪	⚪	⚪	⚪

17 Ray has collected 199 stamps.

He added another 49 stamps to his collection.

How many stamps has he now?

249	250	248	247
⚪	⚪	⚪	⚪

18 In a movie theatre are 300 people.

169 are children.

How many are NOT children?

Write your answer in the box.

---

19 There are 100 students in a library. 77 of the students are boys.

What percentage of the students are girls?

    23%   24%   33%   32%
     ◯   ◯   ◯   ◯

---

20 Leonard began reading a book at 2.35. She finished reading the book in 80 minutes.

What time did he finish reading the book?

    3:55   3:15   3:50   3:45
     ◯   ◯   ◯   ◯

---

21 Henrietta made 150 cards. He placed the cards into packets.

Each packet contained 8 cards.

How many cards are left over?

    5   7   8   6
    ◯   ◯   ◯   ◯

22 Four stopwatch times for a race are compared.

Which stopwatch shows the fastest time?

Shade one bubble

◯ | 01:2:03 |

◯ | 01:2:12 |

◯ | 01:2:11 |

◯ | 01:2:10 |

23 A book costs $19.50. Adam has a $50 note to pay for it.

How much change should he receive when he buys the book?

Write your answer in the box.

$ [   ]

24 Tammy bought 21 stamps. Mark bought 17.

Emma bought 19. Paul bought 18.

How many stamps did they buy altogether?

| 75 | 74 | 76 | 73 |
| ◯ | ◯ | ◯ | ◯ |

25 The cost of 3 books is $24. Two of the books cost $9.50 each.

How much does the third book cost?

$4.90	$6.00	$5.10	$5.00
◯	◯	◯	◯

26 A box is half full of oranges.

All oranges are the same size.

After another 45 oranges are added to the box, the box is

three quarters full.

How many oranges will the box hold when it is full?

170	190	160	180
◯	◯	◯	◯

27 **Which one of these algorithms does NOT involve trading?**

+ 407	+ 630	+ 498	+ 517
673	408	105	370
──	──	──	──
──	──	──	──
◯	◯	◯	◯

28 An insect has 6 legs.

Georgia wishes to draw 9 insects.

How many legs will Georgia need to draw altogether?

48   63   54   55

◯   ◯   ◯   ◯

29 Henry is 190 cm tall.

His sister is half Henry's height.

How tall is Henry's sister?

Write your answer in the box.

[   ] cm

30 Alice measured part of her school playground.

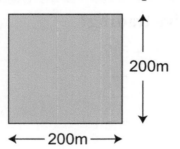

200m

←— 200m —→

What is the area of the part of the playground she measured?

400 m²   4000 m²   40 m²   40 000 m²

◯   ◯   ◯   ◯

31 Des used a scale of 1 cm = 1 km to show the distance between his home and his school.

0.5 cm

home ←——————————————————→ school

What is the real distance between Des's home and his school?

ANSWER = [ ] km

32

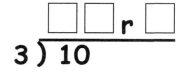

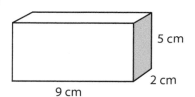

33

This container is 9 cm long, 2cm wide and 5cm deep.

What is the volume of water in the container when it is half full?

45 cm³   900 m³   90 m³   100 m³

○   ○   ○   ○

34 Which rectangle would have a perimeter of 16 cm and an area of 15 cm²?

Shade one bubble

○ a rectangle of 4 cm × 4 cm

○ a rectangle of 6 cm × 3 cm

○ a rectangle of 6 cm × 2 cm

○ a rectangle of 5 cm × 3 cm

35 Kim walked around a field three times.

The first time took 10 minutes.

The other walks took 1½ minute longer than the walk before.

How long did 3 walks take?

☐ minutes

36

Bus Time Table	
First Bus	6.55 a.m.
Second Bus	7.50 a.m.
Third Bus	8.45 a.m.
Fourth Bus	☐

These are the times that buses pass a bus stop.

The same amount of time is between the arrival of each bus.

When will the next bus come?

9.20 a.m.   9.30 a.m.   9.35 a.m.   9.40 a.m.

○   ○   ○   ○

37 A piece of wood has a mass of 5050 grams.

5050 grams is the same as

0.5050 kg	50.50 kg	5.050 kg	505.0 kg
⬭	⬭	⬭	⬭

38 A tap drips 10 mL every 1½ minutes.

How long will it take to drip a litre of water?

⬭ 1½ minutes

⬭ 125 minutes

⬭ 50 minutes

⬭ 150 minutes

39 **The number that is 900 less than 1005 is**

95	105	950	115
⬭	⬭	⬭	⬭

40 A wall is 9.5 metres long.

This is the same as

⬭ 90½ cm

⬭ 9½ cm

⬭ 950 cm

⬭ 900 cm

41 What is the smallest number you can make by changing the order of these numbers?

Shade one bubble

| 8 | 0 | 1 | 2 |

Write your answer in the box below.

42 Ulle is counting backwards by 9s.

108, 99, ☐ , ☐ , ☐ , 63

Which number should go here?

72   73   71   70
○   ○   ○   ○

43 Lionel had a 450 mL carton of juice.

He drank half of the juice.

How much juice did Lionel drink?

○ 125 mL

○ 220 mL

○ 225 mL

44 **What fraction of the grid is shaded?**

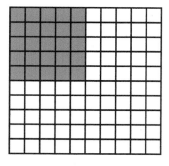

- ⬭ 26 out of 100
- ⬭ 75 out of 100
- ⬭ 24 out of 100
- ⬭ 25 out of 100

45 **Colour in the date on the calendar that is exactly three weeks before 8th October.**

SEPTEMBER						
MON	**TUES**	**WED**	**THU**	**FRI**	**SAT**	**SUN**
		1	2	3	4	5
6	7	8	9	10	11	12
13	14	15	16	17	18	19
20	21	22	23	24	25	26
27	28	29	30			

OCTOBER						
MON	**TUES**	**WED**	**THU**	**FRI**	**SAT**	**SUN**
				1	2	3
4	5	6	7	8	9	10
11	12	13	14	15	16	17
18	19	20	21	22	23	24
25	26	27	28	29	30	31

46 Robert counted 201 seagulls at a beach. 149 flew off.

How many seagulls were still there?

Shade one bubble

61	41	52	51
○	○	○	○

47 A book has 255 pages. Roberta has read 199 pages.

How many more pages has Roberta left to read before she has finished the book?

60	55	57	56
○	○	○	○

48 Daisy wishes to buy four items. The items have these prices.

97c	33c	93c	37c

Daisy will need

○ more than $2.60

○ exactly $2.60

○ less than $2.60

1 Look at this grid.

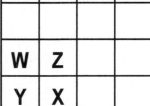

What position is **Y** in?

A3   A1   A4   A2

○   ○   ○   ○

Shade one bubble

2 **Terry had 119 coloured pencils.**

He gave 69 to his sister.

How many coloured pencils did Terry have left?

Write your answer in the box.

3 Greta has 175 cards. Sharon has twice as many cards as Greta.

How many cards does Sharon have?

375   350   450   275

○   ○   ○   ○

4 Dad bought a pen for 95c and a book for $10.95.

What change should Dad receive from $20.00?

$9.10 $10.10 $8.10 $10.90

○   ○   ○   ○

5   A clock looks like this.

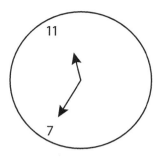

Which one of the times below is the same time as the clock above?

| 11:25 | 12:35 | 11:35 | 11:40 |

    ○   ○   ○   ○

6   A tree is 3000 cm high.

3000 cm is

○ more than 30 metres

○ equal to 30 metres

○ less than 30 metres

7   **Which one of these number sentences is NOT correct?**

○ 8 x 8 = 64

○ 7 x 8 = 55

○ 5 x 8 = 40

○ 8 x 9 = 72

8   **What is the answer to this number sentence?**

70 + 50 + 90 + 80 = ☐

9   A car's fuel gauge shows full when the tank has 36 litres of petrol in it.

Shade one bubble

About how many litres of petrol are shown by the arrow in the car's fuel guage?

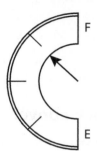

21	28	27	24
○	○	○	○

10   Bryon has a choice between these buys.

Which is the cheapest buy?

- ○ 49 cents each
- ○ 5 for two dollars
- ○ 4 for two dollars
- ○ 51 cents each

11   Two groups visited the zoo.

One group had 159 people. The other group had 99 people.

How many people were in the two groups?

Write your answer in the box.

12 This is the time on Jeremy's watch.

| 12:29 |

This is the time on Jack's watch.

| 1:05 |

What is the difference between the two times?

35 minutes   36 minutes   37 minutes   31 minutes

◯   ◯   ◯   ◯

13 **What is the area of this shape?**

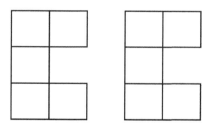

10 squares   9 squares   11 squares   8 squares

◯   ◯   ◯   ◯

14 **Colour three quarters of this shape.**

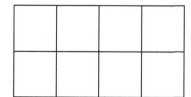

15 9 + 41 + 1 + 49 = ☐

Shade one bubble

The answer to this number sentence is equal to

110   100   105   50

○   ○   ○   ○

---

16 Books are on sale 2 for $15.

Casey paid $45 for her books.

How many books did Casey buy?

5   7   6   8

○   ○   ○   ○

---

17 Royce has collected 107 stamps.

He added another 49 stamps to his collection.

How many stamps has he now?

154   153   155   156

○   ○   ○   ○

18 In a movie theatre are 250 people.

189 are children.

How many are NOT children?

Write your answer in the box.

---

19 There are 100 students in a library. 100 of the students are boys.

What percentage of the students are girls?

2%	0%	1%	100%
◯	◯	◯	◯

---

20 John began reading a book at 4.50. He finished reading the book in 100 minutes.

What time did he finish reading the book?

6:30	5:30	6:25	6:35
◯	◯	◯	◯

---

21 Harold made 150 cards. He placed the cards into packets. Each packet contained 9 cards.

How many cards are left over?

5	7	8	6
◯	◯	◯	◯

22 Four stopwatch times for a race are compared.

Which stopwatch shows the fastest time?

Shade one bubble

○ | 02:1:03 |

○ | 02:1:02 |

○ | 02:2:01 |

○ | 02:1:01 |

---

23 A book costs $16.50. Harry has a $50 note to pay for it.

How much change should he receive when he buys the book?

Write your answer in the box.

$ [   ]

---

24 Tessa bought 19 stamps. Chris bought 23.

Rene bought 17. Paul bought 23.

How many stamps did they buy altogether?

82	80	83	81
○	○	○	○

25 The cost of 3 books is $25. Two of the books cost $7.50 each.

How much does the third book cost?

$9.50 $10.00 $10.50 $11.00

⬭   ⬭   ⬭   ⬭

---

26 A box is half full of oranges.

All oranges are the same size.

After another 35 oranges are added to the box, the box is

three quarters full.

How many oranges will the box hold when it is full?

150   160   140   240

⬭   ⬭   ⬭   ⬭

---

27 **Which one of these algorithms does NOT involve trading?**

+ 307	+ 630	+ 808	+ 447
678	309	104	360
───	───	───	───
───	───	───	───

⬭   ⬭   ⬭   ⬭

Shade one bubble

28 An insect has 6 legs.

Gina wishes to draw 12 insects.

How many legs will Gina need to draw altogether?

69	70	71	72
○	○	○	○

29 Robert is 185 cm tall.

His sister is half Robert's height.

How tall is Robert's sister?

Write your answer in the box.

[____] cm

30 Peta measured part of her school playground.

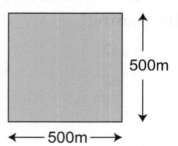
500m
←— 500m —→

What is the area of the part of the playground she measured?

1000 m²	25 000 m²	250 m²	250 000 m²
○	○	○	○

31 Doug used a scale of 1 cm = 1 km to show the distance between his home and his school.

0.25 cm

home ←——————————————→ school

What is the real distance between Doug's home and his school?

ANSWER = [   ] km

32

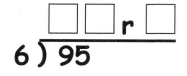

33

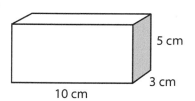

This container is 10 cm long, 3 cm wide and 5 cm deep.

What is the volume of water in the container when it is half full?

80 cm³   75 m³   150 m³   60 m³
○   ○   ○   ○

34 Which rectangle would have a perimeter of 22 cm and an area of 28 cm²?

Shade one bubble

○ a rectangle of 6 cm × 4 cm

○ a rectangle of 7 cm × 3 cm

○ a rectangle of 8 cm × 4 cm

○ a rectangle of 7 cm × 4 cm

35 Kathy walked around a field three times.

The first time took 5 minutes.

The other walks took 2½ minute longer than the walk before.

How long did 3 walks take?

| | minutes

36

Bus Time Table	
First Bus	6.25 a.m.
Second Bus	7.15 a.m.
Third Bus	8.05 a.m.
Fourth Bus	

These are the times that buses pass a bus stop.

The same amount of time is between the arrival of each bus.

When will the next bus come?

  9.55 a.m.   8.50 a.m.   9.00 a.m.   8.55 a.m.

    ○   ○   ○   ○

37 A piece of wood has a mass of 50 grams.

50 grams is the same as

0.50 kg	50.00 kg	0.05 kg	5.00 kg
⬭	⬭	⬭	⬭

38 A tap drips 20 mL every 5 minutes.

How long will it take to drip a litre of water?

○ 350 minutes

○ 150 minutes

○ 250 minutes

○ 200 minutes

39 The number that is 500 less than 1050 is

450	550	650	500
⬭	⬭	⬭	⬭

40 A wall is 7.00 metres long.

This is the same as

○ 70 cm

○ 7 cm

○ 700 cm

○ 7000 cm

41 **What is the smallest number you can make by changing the order of these numbers?**

| 3 | 0 | 0 | 2 |

Write your answer in the box below.

Shade one bubble

42 Aaron is counting backwards by 7s.

106, 99, ☐ , ☐ , ☐ , 71

Which number should go here?

| 85 | 84 | 87 | 86 |
| ○ | ○ | ○ | ○ |

43 Jenny had a 950 mL carton of juice.

She drank half of the juice.

How much juice did Jenny drink?

○ 465 mL

○ 475 mL

○ 470 mL

44 **What fraction of the grid is shaded?**

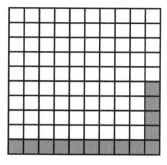

- ⬭ 12 out of 100
- ⬭ 5 out of 100
- ⬭ 14 out of 100
- ⬭ 7 out of 100

45 **Colour in the date on the calendar that is exactly three weeks before 17th October.**

SEPTEMBER						
MON	TUES	WED	THU	FRI	SAT	SUN
		1	2	3	4	5
6	7	8	9	10	11	12
13	14	15	16	17	18	19
20	21	22	23	24	25	26
27	28	29	30			

OCTOBER						
MON	TUES	WED	THU	FRI	SAT	SUN
				1	2	3
4	5	6	7	8	9	10
11	12	13	14	15	16	17
18	19	20	21	22	23	24
25	26	27	28	29	30	31

46 Robyn counted 141 seagulls at a beach. 93 flew off.

How many seagulls were still there?

Shade one bubble

48	49	50	547
◯	◯	◯	◯

47 A book has 205 pages. Samuel has read 99 pages.

How many more pages has Samuel left to read before he has finished the book?

106	105	107	104
◯	◯	◯	◯

48 Damian wishes to buy four items. The items have these prices.

77c	33c	77c	33c

Damian will need

◯ more than $2.20

◯ exactly $2.20

◯ less than $2.20

Year 5 Numeracy
NAPLAN*-Format Practice Tests

TEST 1
(pp.4 – 19)

1   W

2   35

3   16

4   80c

5   40

6   more than 1 metre

7   7 x 3 = 20 (should be 7 x 3 = 21)

8   Circle $1, 50c, 20c, 20c, 10c

9

10   less than a minute

11   Tan is opposite Mary.

12   3; (50c + 10c + 10c + 10c)

13   16 squares

14   Colour in 2 eighths (i.e. sections).

15   A and B

16

17   129

18   J

19   44%

20   9:10

21   1

22   Jack

23   $21

24   James

25   12

26   about 4½ kg

27   + 254
      305

28   Use centimetres to measure the distance across a large river.

29   69 cm

30   400 m²

31   8

32   23 r 1

33   e.g. a rectangle 4 cm long and 3 cm wide.

34   About 41°

35   499

36   7.50 a.m.

37   1.438 kg

38   200 minutes

39   15906

40   a sphere

41   9532

42   85

43

44   33 out of 100

45   Colour in 9th October

46   36

47   height

48   less than $3.00

TEST 2
(pp.20−35)

1 X

2 18

3 48

4 50c

5 45

6 less than 2 metres

7 7 x 4 = 29 (should be 7 x 4 = 28)

8 Circle $1, 50c, 50c, 20c, 20c, 10c

9

10 more than a minute

11 Lim is opposite Margaret.

12 2; (50c + 20c + 20c)

13 20 squares

14 Colour in 6 eighths (i.e. sections).

15 A and B

16

17 119

18 P

19 39%

20 9:05

21 1

22 Tony

23 $23

24 Henry

25 8

26 about 7½ kg

27 + 253

     424

28 Use grams to measure the weight of a large truck.

29 71 cm

30 900 m²

31 11

32 26 r 2

33 e.g. a rectangle 6 cm long and 1 cm wide or 5 cm long and 2 cm wide.

34 About 104°

35 420

36 7.40 a.m.

37 3.469 kg

38 1000 minutes

39 20506

40 a cylinder

41 8740

42 88

43

44 27 out of 100

45 Colour in 11th October

46 47

47 height

48 exactly $2.50

TEST 3
(pp.36 – 51)

1 W

2 29

3 78

4 60c

5 55

6 equal to 1½ metres

7 8 x 5 = 41 (should be 8 x 5 = 40)

8 Colour $1, 50c, 50c, 20c, 10c

9

10 10 cents each

11 56

12 40 minutes

13 15 squares

14 Colour 4 eighths or half of the shape.

15 A and C

16

17 114

18 V

19 61%

20 8:40

21 4

22 25

23 $26.50

24 25

25 9

26 about 10½ kg

27 + 203
424

28 Use kilometres to measure the mass of a book (should be kg).

29 58 cm

30 3600 m²

31 25½ or 25.5

32 17 r 2

33 Draw a rectangle 6 cm long and 5 cm wide.

34 180° (2 right angles, back to back)

35 425

36 9.20 a.m.

37 2.409 kg

38 20 minutes

39 17 006

40 a hemisphere

41 9930

42 76

43

44 7 out of 100

45 Colour in 14th October

46 59

47 perimeter

48 exactly $2.40

TEST 4
(pp.52–67)

1 W

2 29

3 114

4 62c

5 60

6 more than 1½ metres

7 11 x 5 = 50 (should be 11 x 5 = 55)

8 Circle $2, $2, $1, 50c, 20c, 10c

9

10 5 for one dollar

11 62

12 40 minutes

13 13 squares

14 Colour 6 eighths or sections of the shape.

15 A and C

16

17 116

18 H

19 59%

20 9:50

21 2

22 28

23 $22.50

24 33

25 12

26 about 1½ kg

27 + 391
  308

28 Use grams to measure the amount of medicine in a tiny glass (should be mL).

29 59 cm

30 4900 m²

31 17½ or 17.5

32 22 r 2

33 A rectangle 5 cm long and 5 cm wide or 6 cm long and 4 cm wide.

34 90°

35 410

36 8.05 a.m.

37 2.739 kg

38 50 minutes

39 9006

40 a cone

41 9853

42 79

43

44 11 out of 100

45 Colour 10th October

46 49

47 perimeter

48 more than $2.70

TEST 5
(pp.68–83)

1 Z

2 48

3 158

4 16c

5 45

6 more than 3½ metres

7 8 x 7 = 57 (should be 8 x 7 = 56)

8 Circle $2, $2, $1, 50c, 20c, 10c, 10c

9 20

10 4 for one dollar

11 86

12 35 minutes

13 9 squares

14 Colour 8 eighths or all of the shape.

15 70

16 8

17 117

18 C

19 19%

20 9:30

21 4

22 00:1:25

23 $16.50

24 35

25

26 about 12 kg

27 + 320

471

28 Use grams to measure the volume of a glass of water (should be cm^3).

29 61

30 6400 m^2

31 7½ or 7.5

32 12 r 6

33 A rectangle 5 cm long and 1 cm wide **or** 4 cm long and 2 cm wide **or** 3 cm long and 3 cm wide.

34 About 66°

35 420

36 9.25 a.m.

37 4.039 kg

38 150 minutes

39 19 105

40 a triangular pyramid

41 9761

42 73

43 a quarter of a litre

44 55 out of 100

45 Colour in 4th October

46 49

47 221

48 more than $3.00

TEST 6
(pp.84 – 99)

1	W	**26**	100
2	67	**27**	+ 390
3	116		408
4	20c	**28**	32
5	40	**29**	66 cm
6	equal to 6½ metres	**30**	8100 m²
7	8 x 9 = 63 (should be 8 x 9 = 72)	**31**	1¾ or 1.75
8	Circle $2, $1, 50c, 20c	**32**	11 r 3
9	60	**33**	32 cm³
10	4 for one dollar	**34**	a rectangle 5 cm x 4 cm
11	67	**35**	5 + 6 + 7 = 18
12	55 minutes	**36**	9.30 a.m.
13	11 squares	**37**	7.045 kg
14	Colour 3 eighths or sections of the shape.	**38**	15 minutes
15	73	**39**	1005
16	20	**40**	800 cm
17	125	**41**	1356
18	J	**42**	73
19	51%	**43**	half a litre
20	9:40	**44**	11 out of 100
21	0	**45**	Colour in 19th September
22	00:0:18	**46**	64
23	$20.50	**47**	71
24	35	**48**	less than $3.50
25	▷		

TEST 7
(pp.100 – 115)

1 D1	**26** 200
2 44	**27** + 307
3 134	671
4 10c	**28** 56
5 10 votes	**29** 72½ or 72.5
6 equal to 10½ metres	**30** 10 000 m²
7 7 x 8 = 57 (should be 7 x 8 = 56)	**31** 15½ or 15.5
8 Circle $2, $1, 50c, 20c, 10c, 5c	**32** 13 r 2
9 45	**33** 18 cm³
10 30 cents each	**34** a rectangle 6 cm x 3 cm
11 143	**35** 7 + 8 + 9 = 24
12 55 minutes	**36** 9.20 a.m.
13 11 squares	**37** 9.055 kg
14 Colour 5 eighths or sections	**38** 25 minutes
of the shape.	**39** 905
15 90	**40** 750 cm
16 10	**41** 6789
17 155	**42** 76
18 90	**43** 375 mL
19 43%	**44** 15 out of 100
20 1:40	**45** Colour in 20th September
21 2	**46** 55
22 00:2:28	**47** 63
23 $23.50	**48** less than $3.95
24 42	
25 $7	

TEST 8
(pp.116 – 131)

1	C2	**26**	300
2	39	**27**	+ 490
3	198		408
4	5c	**28**	72
5	15 – 0 = 15 votes	**29**	75
6	less than 15½ metres	**30**	2500 m²
7	7 x 6 = 43 (should be 7 x 6 = 42)	**31**	10½ or 10.5
8	57	**32**	16 r 2
9	15	**33**	28 cm³
10	2 for 90 cents	**34**	a rectangle 6 cm x 4 cm
11	193	**35**	8 + 8½ + 9 = 25½
12	6 minutes	**36**	9.40 a.m.
13	9 squares	**37**	5.555 kg
14	Colour 7 eighths or sections of the shape.	**38**	35 minutes
15	80	**39**	955
16	10	**40**	550 cm
17	168	**41**	5079 (the number cannot begin with 0)
18	180	**42**	79
19	83%	**43**	175 mL
20	10:55	**44**	12 out of 100
21	3	**45**	Colour in 10th September
22	00:2:09	**46**	91
23	$28.50	**47**	131
24	35	**48**	exactly $2.00
25	$6.00		

TEST 9
(pp.132 – 147)

1 A4	**26** 180
2 30	**27** + 517
3 178	370
4 36c	**28** 54
5 6:15	**29** 95
6 equal to 25 metres	**30** 40 000 m²
7 8 x 9 = 74 (should be 8 x 9 = 72)	**31** ½ or 0.5
8 200	**32** 03 r 1
9 36	**33** 45 cm³
10 5 for one dollar	**34** a rectangle 5 cm x 3 cm
11 118	**35** 10 + 11½ + 13 = 34½
12 56 minutes	**36** 9.40 a.m.
13 11 squares	**37** 5.050 kg
14 Colour in 2 eighths or sections of the shape.	**38** 150 minutes
	39 105
15 200	**40** 950 cm
16 10	**41** 1028
17 248	**42** 72
18 131	**43** 225 mL
19 23%	**44** 25 out of 100
20 3:55	**45** Colour in 17th September
21 6	**46** 52
22 01:2:03	**47** 56
23 $30.50	**48** exactly $2.60
24 75	
25 $5.00	

TEST 10
(pp.148 – 163)

1	A1	**26**	140
2	50	**27**	+ 630
3	350		309
4	$8.10	**28**	72
5	11:35	**29**	92½
6	equal to 30 metres	**30**	250 000 m²
7	7 x 8 = 55	**31**	¼ or 0.25
8	290	**32**	15 r 5
9	27	**33**	75 cm³
10	5 for two dollars	**34**	a rectangle 7 cm x 4 cm
11	258	**35**	5 + 7½ + 10 = 22½
12	36 minutes	**36**	8.55 a.m.
13	10 squares	**37**	0.05 kg
14	Colour in 6 eighths or sections of the shape.	**38**	250 minutes
15	100	**39**	550
16	6	**40**	700 cm
17	156	**41**	2003
18	61	**42**	85
19	0%	**43**	475 mL
20	6:30	**44**	14 out of 100
21	6	**45**	Colour in 26th September
22	02:1:01	**46**	48
23	$33.50	**47**	106
24	82	**48**	exactly $2.20
25	$10.00		